Great Hands I Wish I Had Played

Raymond & Sally Brock

B. T. Batsford, *London*

First published 2002

© Raymond & Sally Brock 2002

ISBN 0 7134 8798 4

Typeset by Wakewing, High Wycombe
Printed by Creative Print & Design, Ebbw Vale, Wales
for the publishers,
B. T. Batsford, 64 Brewery Road,
London N7 9NT

A member of **Chrysalis** Books plc

A BATSFORD BRIDGE BOOK
Series Editor: Phil King

CONTENTS

INTRODUCTION

The hands in this book can be divided into two groups: those one of us had a chance to make at the table but didn't, and those that were not dealt to either of us but we wish had been – at least after the event when we had worked out how to play them. Some of the hands in this latter category were made at the table and some were not. What all the hands have in common is that we wish we could add them to our fairly small folder of personal well-played hands.

All the write-ups are in the first person singular (despite the co-authorship), as if we had made them at the table, because surely that makes for a better story. But in small print at the end is 'the truth'.

In some cases we have tinkered with the hands a little. Since this is a book about cardplay we do not want to distract the reader with a lot of abstruse bidding sequences, so we have often changed the bidding to a straightforward Acol auction. But in doing this we have had to be careful to ensure that the same inferences are available as there were at the table. In a very few cases, simple Acol could not have led to the same contract, played by the same hand with the same inferences; in these cases we have either left the actual bidding, or occasionally changed the suits around.

This is a book to read and enjoy rather than to study, but we would be surprised if you did not learn something at the same time.

Most of the matchpoints

The bidding

I am playing in the semi-final of the World Women's Pairs. As North, in fourth seat with both sides vulnerable, I pick up a good hand:

♠ A86
♡ A75
◇ AQ864
♣ Q7

My left-hand opponent opens one club, partner passes and my right-hand opponent responds one heart. I have a choice of actions now: I could pass, bid two diamonds or one no-trump. I am playing match-pointed pairs so I decide on one no-trump which describes my balanced hand quite well. This is followed by two passes and my right-hand opponent bids two clubs. It is rarely best to allow the opponents to play at a low level at pairs so I now bid two diamonds. I am pleased when opener presses on to three clubs, but not so happy when partner competes to three diamonds. This ends the auction.

The bidding has been:

West	North	East	South
1♣	Pass	1♡	1NT
Pass	Pass	2♣	2◇
3♣	3◇	All Pass	

The play

West leads the ace of clubs and this is what I can see:

♠ 72
♡ K64
♢ 107532
♣ 862

♠ A86
♡ A75
♢ AQ864
♣ Q7

West cashes the ace and king of clubs, East following upwards, and switches to the ten of hearts.

Partner doesn't have a great deal but what she has fits quite well. It looks as though the contract depends on the diamond finesse, but that figures to be wrong in light of West's opening – they generally bid soundly in North America.

What other chances are there? The king of diamonds might be bare, though that is unlikely since West won't have five spades and she would have bid two hearts on the third round with three. I know that West is short in hearts, so maybe I can eliminate the other suits and throw West in with the king of diamonds. The alternative is simply to play East for the king of diamonds and take the finesse. However, if I am right about West not having a singleton diamond, if East does have the king of diamonds it will be singleton and that will show up.

I win the heart in hand just in case East has six – I don't want to risk getting one of my heart winners ruffed – and duck a spade. East wins and plays another heart. I win the king, cash the ace of diamonds, play the ace of spades and ruff a spade, and then ruff dummy's last club in my hand. Now I exit with a diamond and am pleased when West wins and has to give me a ruff and discard.

The full deal:

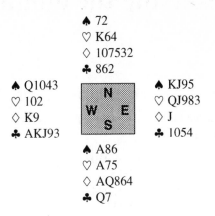

♠ 72
♡ K64
◇ 107532
♣ 862

♠ Q1043
♡ 102
◇ K9
♣ AKJ93

♠ KJ95
♡ QJ983
◇ J
♣ 1054

♠ A86
♡ A75
◇ AQ864
♣ Q7

Post mortem

A 5-5 fit is very powerful and in the end the hand played itself. Looking at all four hands, the defence could never set up a heart winner whilst East had an entry, even on a heart lead.

Note that the pre-emptive effect of my one no-trump bid succeeded in causing East/West to miss their best major-suit fit – they can make nine tricks in spades.

The truth: In this book there are going to be plenty of examples of hands I didn't play well, so I thought I would start with quite an easy hand on which I managed to succeed. I played the above hand exactly as stated in the World Women's Pairs held in Montréal in 2002. My partner, Margaret James, and I qualified comfortably for the final – the top 32 pairs in the world – but eventually finished nearer the bottom than the top.

Reversing the dummy

The bidding

Sitting South in second seat, vulnerable against not, in a Gold Cup match, I pick up the following:

♠ AQ104
♡ 85
◇ KQ74
♣ Q73

My right-hand opponent passes and I open one no-trump (12–14). West bids two clubs which is alerted. It transpires that this shows the majors, and partner now bids two spades.

We have the agreement that when the opponents come in over our one no-trump with a bid that shows two specific suits, a bid of either of their suits shows the other two suits, the lower cue-bid being weakish while the higher is game-forcing. So here partner has game-forcing values with both minors. My right-hand opponent passes and I must decide what to do.

While I have spades well guarded, my hearts leave something to be desired. I decide on the straightforward action of showing my four-card diamond suit. Partner now bids three hearts. I take this to mean that he has something in hearts and wants to know if I have a spade stopper, so I oblige him with three no-trumps. However, he now continues with four diamonds. He is clearly interested in a slam and I am not unsuitable. The least I can do is show him the ace of spades. Over my four spades, he continues with five clubs. It is not clear exactly what he wants from me but I like my hand – my trumps are good and it looks as if the queen of clubs is working. I accept his invitation and jump to six diamonds.

The bidding has been:

West	North	East	South
–	–	Pass	1NT
2♣	2♠	Pass	3◇
Pass	3♡	Pass	3NT
Pass	4◇	Pass	4♠
Pass	5♣	Pass	6◇
All Pass			

The play

West leads the ace of hearts and this is what I can see:

♠ 7
♡ K104
◇ AJ1053
♣ AK42

♠ AQ104
♡ 85
◇ KQ74
♣ Q73

I am happy with the dummy and partner's bidding – the ace of hearts was likely with West on the bidding. I need to count my tricks: one spade, one heart, five diamond tricks in dummy and one ruff in hand, and three top clubs. That's eleven but I'll make twelve if diamonds are 2-2 or clubs 3-3. Can I improve on this and cater for bad breaks?

What I need to do is make an extra trump trick. How about ruffing spades in dummy? If I can make four trumps in my hand and three ruffs in the dummy that brings the total trump tricks up to seven, or twelve in all. I seem to have plenty of entries. but the key to a dummy reversal is to start on the ruffs straight away.

On the ace of hearts, East plays the two (showing an odd number), and West continues with a second heart which I win in dummy with the king. I play a spade to the ace and ruff a spade. Now I cash the ace of diamonds, play a diamond to the king (East showing out), ruff another spade, play a club to the queen and take another spade ruff. All I need do now is ruff a heart back to hand, draw the last trump and cash dummy's remaining two club winners for twelve tricks in total.

The full deal:

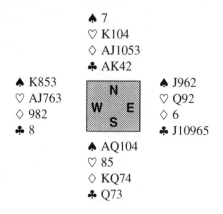

♠ 7
♥ K104
♦ AJ1053
♣ AK42

♠ K853
♥ AJ763
♦ 982
♣ 8

♠ J962
♥ Q92
♦ 6
♣ J10965

♠ AQ104
♥ 85
♦ KQ74
♣ Q73

Post mortem

Dummy reversals are often difficult to spot. Suppose declarer fails to ruff a spade immediately, and instead draws trumps. Is there a way for him to recover?

When declarer discovers the 3-1 trump break, he knows that clubs cannot break 3-3, for West is known to have major-suit length. He can still succeed if he plays for East to have the jack of spades. What he must do is play the ace of spades and then the queen, running it if West plays low. But West will surely cover, as he is marked with the king of spades for his two club bid – had East held it he would surely have doubled North's two spade cue-bid. East has discarded a club and a heart on two trumps and the position is:

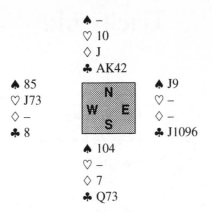

♠ –
♡ 10
◇ J
♣ AK42

♠ 85
♡ J73
◇ –
♣ 8

♠ J9
♡ –
◇ –
♣ J1096

♠ 104
♡ –
◇ 7
♣ Q73

When declarer now ruffs a heart in hand, East is squeezed. His best choice is a spade, but now declarer can ruff a spade in dummy to bring down the jack (or he could cross to dummy's ace of clubs and simply play the last trump which would squeeze East in the black suits).

The truth: In actual play I was defending in an early round of the Gold Cup. The deal was a comedy of errors, with South and East both trying to play more badly than the other. In the event, East won this particular contest and the slam made.

Tricky bid

The bidding

First in hand at Game All, I pick up the following:

♠ QJ4
♡ Q9853
◇ A6
♣ A43

This sort of hand is tricky when playing Acol with a weak no-trump. If I open one heart I will have to rebid two hearts if partner responds two diamonds, and I don't have a wonderful rebid if partner responds in a black suit, though it would probably be best to raise him. I prefer to open one no-trump on these balanced hands with honours in all suits, even if I do have a five-card major.

After my one no-trump opening, partner responds two clubs, Stayman, but East sticks his oar in with a leap to three diamonds. I ask whether this is a strong or a weak bid and am told that in principle it is weak, but obviously won't be too weak vulnerable. Maybe I should pass now in case partner is weak, but I like my hand so I risk bidding three hearts, and partner raises me to four.

The bidding has been:

West	North	East	South
–	–	–	1NT
Pass	2♣	3◇	3♡
Pass	4♡	All Pass	

The play

West leads the four of diamonds and this is what I can see:

♠ A1063
♡ AJ74
◇ 73
♣ J62

♠ QJ4
♡ Q9853
◇ A6
♣ A43

I see that partner has been a little frisky, issuing a game invitation with a balanced 10-count. However, four hearts looks to have play, particularly as it is quite likely that West has both major-suit kings. I win the ace of diamonds and run the queen of hearts, but this loses to East's king. East cashes a top diamond, West showing out, and switches to the ten of clubs. Obviously this could be a singleton, but it is more likely that East's singleton is in one of the majors, so I decide to duck. West wins with the queen and plays a trump. I win the ace of trumps, East showing out, and cash the jack. The position now is:

♠ A1063
♡ 7
◇ –
♣ J6

♠ QJ4
♡ 98
◇ –
♣ A4

East's distribution seems to be 2-1-8-2, which is a pity as it looks as if I need spades to be 3-3.

No, I don't, of course I don't. I can squeeze West in the black suits. I simply play two more rounds of trumps. On the last one West cannot keep two clubs and four spades. He lets go a spade and now I take the spade finesse, making four tricks in the suit for my contract.

The full deal:

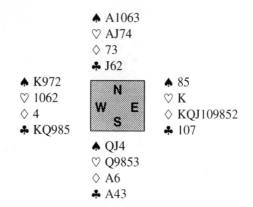

```
                    ♠ A1063
                    ♡ AJ74
                    ◇ 73
                    ♣ J62
   ♠ K972                        ♠ 85
   ♡ 1062          N             ♡ K
   ◇ 4         W       E         ◇ KQJ109852
   ♣ KQ985          S            ♣ 107
                    ♠ QJ4
                    ♡ Q9853
                    ◇ A6
                    ♣ A43
```

The truth: In truth, the auction did not quite go like this. I did open one no-trump as South and North did use Stayman, but at the table East bid four diamonds, not three diamonds. When this was passed to North he passed it out, because he thought that if he doubled it was too likely that I would remove to four of a major which would not make. In the event we collected 200 from four diamonds for the only plus score on our cards in a team of eight match.

Squeezing dummy

The bidding

I am sitting West in the Portland Pairs (English National Mixed Pairs) when I pick up the following unexciting collection, vulnerable against not:

♠ 82
♡ A108
◇ J9854
♣ 852

I pass as dealer, North opens one club, my partner passes, and South responds one diamond. North now rebids one spade and South closes the auction with one no-trump.

The bidding has been:

West	North	East	South
Pass	1♣	Pass	1◇
Pass	1♠	Pass	1NT
All Pass			

The play

What to lead? The unbid suit does not look very attractive (and indeed is often the declaring side's best fit on this type of auction). Eventually I decide to go for a passive lead of dummy's first-bid suit, and choose the five of clubs. Dummy is tabled and this is what I can see:

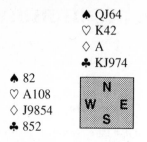

♠ QJ64
♡ K42
◇ A
♣ KJ974

♠ 82
♡ A108
◇ J9854
♣ 852

Declarer plays low from the dummy at trick one, partner contributes the six and declarer wins the ten. She now plays a diamond to dummy's ace, followed by the queen of spades which holds, and a spade to her king. She now cashes the king and queen of diamonds, discarding a club and a heart while partner discards a low heart. Declarer now exits with a spade to the jack and partner's ace while I discard a diamond. This is clearly the position:

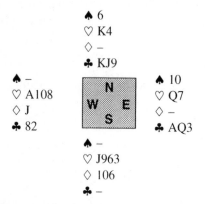

♠ 6
♡ K4
◇ –
♣ KJ9

♠ –
♡ A108
◇ J
♣ 82

♠ 10
♡ Q7
◇ –
♣ AQ3

♠ –
♡ J963
◇ 106
♣ –

Partner cashes the ten of spades and plays a heart to my ace. I now produce the *coup de grâce*, the jack of diamonds. This squeezes the dummy. In practice, declarer threw a club, partner a heart, and now a second club through the dummy produced three tricks in the suit. Had declarer thrown a heart from the dummy, the defence would have taken two hearts and two clubs instead of three clubs and one heart. One down was worth a bushel of matchpoints.

The full deal:

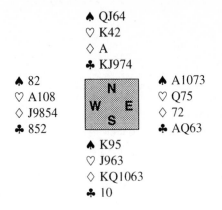

                    ♠ QJ64
                    ♡ K42
                    ◇ A
                    ♣ KJ974

♠ 82   ♠ A1073
♡ A108   N   ♡ Q75
◇ J9854   W   E   ◇ 72
♣ 852   S   ♣ AQ63

                    ♠ K95
                    ♡ J963
                    ◇ KQ1063
                    ♣ 10

Post mortem

Declarer did not play the hand with any great skill. A better plan would have been to try to set up dummy's clubs. After crossing to dummy with the ace of diamonds, she should have played a top club, forcing East to play some other suit. If East plays a diamond, she wins and plays a spade to the queen. As the cards lie she is likely to come to eight tricks.

The truth: In real life partner was not quite on the ball. After cashing the ten of spades in the above ending, he exited, not with his low heart, but with the *queen*. This allows declarer to discard a heart from the dummy when the jack of diamonds is cashed, but she also fell from grace and discarded a club so the contract still went one down, but not as prettily as it should have done.

Helpful bidding

The bidding

First in hand at unfavourable vulnerability, I hear my partner open a weak no-trump. The next hand bids two clubs, showing the majors, and I hold:

♠ AJ93
♡ A
◇ K72
♣ Q10754

I wish to show a good hand and would certainly like to take a penalty from an opposing spade contract, so I start with a double. My left-hand opponent jumps to three hearts and this is passed back to me. Partner's pass encourages me; with heart values he would double, so maybe there is a slam on. The trouble is that although we must have a fit I don't yet know what it is. If I bid my poor club suit, it may deter partner from showing what could be strong diamonds.

I decide to temporise with a cue-bid of the opponents' suit. The worst that can happen is that partner bids a four-card diamond suit, but surely he would not do that unless it was very chunky, in which case the 4-3 fit could even be the best game.

Over my four hearts, partner bids five no-trumps. That is rather exciting. Presumably he has both minors along with a hand that would like to play in slam. I am happy to co-operate with that idea, so bid six clubs.

The bidding has been:

West	North	East	South
–	1NT	2♣	Dble
3♡	Pass	Pass	4♡
Pass	5NT	Pass	6♣
All Pass			

The play

West leads the three of hearts and this is what I can see:

♠ K10
♡ 1054
◇ AJ104
♣ A983

```
    N
  W   E
    S
```

♠ AJ93
♡ A
◇ K72
♣ Q10754

Partner has shown a keen appreciation of his values I see! But I agree with his judgement, although he has only 12 HCP, his hand looks very suitable: nothing at all in hearts, a good doubleton spade honour, and both minor-suit aces with good subsidiary cards.

This is a good slam, especially on the bidding. All I need to do is avoid losing two tricks in the minors.

My best chance of avoiding a club loser is to find East with the singleton jack, so at trick two I play the queen of clubs. West covers with the king, but East does not oblige, simply following with the two.

A bit of ruffing now seems called for. So I ruff a heart back to hand and play three rounds of spades, ruffing the third in the dummy. West turns up with Qxx. I ruff a heart back to hand and play my winning jack of spades.

West discards a heart and I pitch a diamond from the dummy. I now exit with a trump. West wins the jack as East follows, so West's forced diamond exit saves me a guess in the suit.

The full deal:

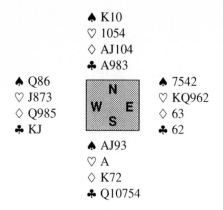

♠ K10
♥ 1054
◊ AJ104
♣ A983

♠ Q86   ♠ 7542
♥ J873   ♥ KQ962
◊ Q985   ◊ 63
♣ KJ   ♣ 62

♠ AJ93
♥ A
◊ K72
♣ Q10754

Post mortem

Note how East/West's aggressive barrage simply succeeded in pushing us into a slam we would not otherwise have bid. Had East passed, I would have used Stayman and settled for three no-trumps when partner did not have four spades. To make three no-trumps I have to guess well in both spades and diamonds.

If, in the ending, one of the defenders had been left with jack doubleton of trumps, they could have won my trump exit and got off play safely with a trump. This would have left me needing to guess the diamonds. However, by then I would have had a complete count of the hand, and would have given myself my best chance of guessing correctly.

The truth: This hand was played in the 2001 Venice Cup by Austria's Terry Weigkricht.

A thin three no-trumps

The bidding

I am sitting in the South seat at Love All when I hear West on my left open two hearts, showing 5–9 HCP and usually a six-card heart suit. North and East both pass and it is my bid.

♠ A53
♡ A1092
◇ 1096
♣ AK8

I can well believe that my best chance of a plus score is to pass out two hearts. Still, hopefully partner has some length somewhere that may mesh well enough with my hand for me to make three no-trumps. I decide to overcall two no-trumps, showing about 15–17 HCP and a balanced hand. In truth, this is something of an overbid because although I have a good double heart stopper and 15 HCP, my 3-4-3-3 distribution is sterile and offers little hope of developing tricks.

The opponents are silent now, but partner responds three clubs, Stayman, and then bids three no-trumps over my three diamond denial.

The bidding has been:

West	North	East	South
2♡	Pass	Pass	2NT
Pass	3♣	Pass	3◇
Pass	3NT	All Pass	

The play

West leads the king of hearts and this is what I can see:

♠ KQ102
♡ 75
◇ K75
♣ J632

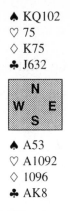

♠ A53
♡ A1092
◇ 1096
♣ AK8

If there had been no opposing bidding I would have been happier with this contract, as it would have been more likely that West held the ace of diamonds or that spades broke. As it is, I will be lucky to make my game.

With no clear plan in mind, it seems a good idea to duck the opening lead. I do this for two reasons: first, it is just possible that West has only five hearts in which case ducking severs the opponents' communications; second, if hearts are 6-1, I can force East to make a discard. If West does not continue hearts, he will have to broach one of the other suits for me.

At trick two West continues with a second top heart, East discarding the three of diamonds. Things are looking up. At least I can play the ten of hearts back (pitching a club from dummy) and establish one more trick. So I do this and West wins while East discards a club.

West thinks for a while and switches to the four of diamonds. This switch is very revealing. Surely West cannot have the semblance of an entry or he would have cleared hearts. I play low on the diamond and East wins with the jack.

East now switches to a club. I have a shrewd suspicion that he holds the queen (otherwise West may have cleared the hearts), but I don't need to risk playing low because East is going to be under intolerable pressure when I cash my established heart. So I rise with the ace of clubs and play the nine of hearts. This is the position with East still to play:

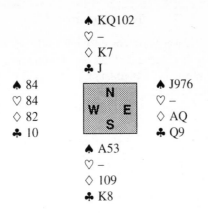

♠ KQ102
♡ –
◊ K7
♣ J

♠ 84
♡ 84
◊ 82
♣ 10

♠ J976
♡ –
◊ AQ
♣ Q9

♠ A53
♡ –
◊ 109
♣ K8

If he discards a club, I know the remaining clubs are 1-1, so I cash the king of clubs and the eight squeezes East again; if he discards a diamond (best), I exit with a low diamond, setting up my king but he is endplayed in any event.

If he discards a diamond on the nine of hearts I exit with a low diamond. He can play the queen of clubs, but when I cash the king of diamonds he is squeezed in the black suits.

If he discards a spade, I cash four rounds of the suit. Now if he throws a low diamond, I throw a club and exit with a low diamond establishing my king. On the other hand, if he throws a club I discard a diamond and cash two club winners.

The full deal:

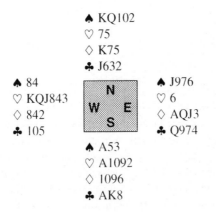

♠ KQ102
♡ 75
◊ K75
♣ J632

♠ 84
♡ KQJ843
◊ 842
♣ 105

♠ J976
♡ 6
◊ AQJ3
♣ Q974

♠ A53
♡ A1092
◊ 1096
♣ AK8

Post mortem

The culprit on the deal was West. Once the king of hearts had been allowed to hold he should have realised that there was no future in continuing the suit, even if his partner had a doubleton. A diamond switch at trick two would have left declarer without resource.

The truth: A hand very similar to this one was misplayed by both declarers in the Women's World Team Olympiad held in 2000 in Maastricht. As stated in the introduction, I have converted most of the sequences in this book to Acol, with a weak no-trump and four-card majors. In reality South was the dealer, but had he opened his four-card suit, West would surely not have been tempted into the misdefence that occurred at the table. Consequently I needed South to be prevented from opening one of his only four-card suit and the only way I could think of to do this was to have West be dealer and open with a weak two-bid. The point of the hand is unchanged.

Baby grand

The bidding

At Love All, I pick up as South:

♠ KQ974
♡ –
◇ A2
♣ AK10963

After two passes, it is my turn and I choose to open a simple one club. Partner responds one heart and I rebid one spade. (In my opinion it is a mistake to crowd the bidding by jumping around, even on very strong hands.) Partner rather surprises me by jumping to three spades. I have very real slam interest now, so I continue with four clubs. He responds with four diamonds which is very good news indeed. I am prepared to have a bash at a small slam, but I don't need much more than four decent trumps along with the king of diamonds I already know about for the grand slam to be good.

I know, I can employ a new-fangled convention, Roman Key Card Voidwood. When one suit is agreed, an unnecessary jump in a new suit shows a void in that suit and asks for aces, partner of course being expected to ignore the ace in the void suit. Accordingly I bid five hearts. Partner responds five no-trumps, showing one or four aces (the king of spades counts as an ace but not the ace of hearts), so I plump for the grand.

The bidding has been:

West	North	East	South
–	Pass	Pass	1♣
Pass	1♡	Pass	1♠
Pass	3♠	Pass	4♣
Pass	4◇	Pass	5♡
Pass	5NT	Pass	7♠
All Pass			

The play

West leads the queen of diamonds and dummy comes down:

♠ A652
♡ J9754
◇ K83
♣ 7

♠ KQ974
♡ –
◇ A2
♣ AK10963

There is rather more work to do here than I had hoped. Still, there are quite good chances. If trumps are 2-2 there should be no problems, so it seems sensible to start by testing spades. Even if East has all four I have some chances so I must start by laying down the ace.

So, I win the ace of diamonds, and play a spade to the ace, both opponents following. I don't want to risk going down in this contract when trumps are 2-2, so I draw a second round of trumps and this time West shows out.

It has got a little tricky. Clearly I can still succeed if clubs are 3-3, or if East has four, or if East has honour doubleton. If I draw a third round of trumps I can never ruff two clubs in the dummy; it is unlikely that I would want to do so (it would need East to be long in both black suits) but I see no reason to give up extra chances. It looks right to lay down my top clubs now and see if I can get any clues.

Both play small on the ace of clubs and on the king East plays the jack. So, it looks as if East does not have four clubs, in which case I am only going to ruff one club in the dummy. So, I draw East's last trump. Now I have to guess whether clubs were 3-3, or whether East started with jack doubleton.

There are two reasons for playing for the latter distribution: first, as East had the longer spades he is likely to have the shorter clubs; secondly, there is the Principle of Restricted Choice which says that I should not play for him to have started with QJx for with that holding he might have played the queen on the second round.

Accordingly, I run the ten of clubs. When East shows out, I ruff the next club in the dummy and claim my grand slam.

The full deal:

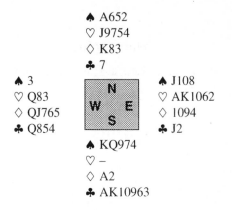

```
              ♠ A652
              ♡ J9754
              ◇ K83
              ♣ 7
♠ 3                         ♠ J108
♡ Q83                       ♡ AK1062
◇ QJ765                     ◇ 1094
♣ Q854                      ♣ J2
              ♠ KQ974
              ♡ —
              ◇ A2
              ♣ AK10963
```

Post mortem

If no club honours had appeared on the second round of the suit (or if West had played an honour on the second round), I would have ruffed a club in the dummy before drawing East's last trump. Had West started with QJxx in clubs I could never succeed, but, by taking a ruff before drawing the last trump, I could cater for East holding four. Notice that if East had indeed started with QJxx in clubs, he would have had the opportunity for a great falsecard by playing an honour on the second round, convincing me to draw his last trump.

The truth: This hand was played in the 2001 World Junior Teams final. In one room Kranyak for the USA finished in six spades. He won the diamond lead, cashed the ace of clubs, ruffed a club, drew trumps and conceded a club. In the other room, Roll, for Israel, finished in the grand slam, played by North. He chose the same line as Kranyak but once he had ruffed a low club at trick three there was no way he could recover.

Foreign adventure

The bidding

Sitting South, in third seat vulnerable against not, I pick up:

♠ AJ943
♡ 76
♢ K
♣ AQ864

My partner opens one heart and East overcalls two clubs. I have a choice now. I could try for a penalty, but at adverse vulnerability this does not seem the right tactic, so I go for the straightforward bid of two spades. Partner jumps to four spades and I decide to go straight to slam.

The bidding has been:

West	North	East	South
–	1♡	2♣	2♠
Pass	4♠	Pass	6♠
All Pass			

The play

West leads the seven of clubs, and this is what I can see:

♠ KQ6
♡ K10852
♢ AQ76
♣ 2

♠ AJ943
♡ 76
♢ K
♣ AQ864

I had hoped that partner would have four spades. As it is there are rather a lot of club losers to deal with. On the other hand I am lucky to have escaped a heart lead for the ace is surely with East.

I take the king of clubs with my ace and cash the king of diamonds. I am going to play on cross-ruff lines but West will be able to discard red-suit cards when I play clubs, so even if the queen of clubs is standing up I don't want to play it just yet. At trick three I play a low club (West following) and ruff with dummy's six of spades. After discarding my two losing hearts on dummy's diamonds I ruff a heart in hand. This is the position:

♠ KQ
♡ K1085
◇ 7
♣ –

♠ AJ94
♡ –
◇ –
♣ Q86

Six more trump tricks will see me home but if I ruff a club West will discard a red suit and I will have to guess how to get back to hand. So I lead the queen of clubs to make West ruff. He ruffs with the two and dummy overruffs. I ruff a heart in hand, West dropping the nine and East the jack, and ruff another club with dummy's last trump, West throwing a diamond. The position is:

♠ –
♡ K108
◇ 7
♣ –

♠ AJ9
♡ –
◇ –
♣ 8

I lead a heart from dummy on which East plays the queen and now I need to think about the opposing distribution. It is clear that West has at least four spades: he is known to have started with two clubs; if I am right that East has the ace of hearts, as he has played the three, jack and queen already, West must have started with a doubleton heart also; and he can have no more than five diamonds.

There are only two genuine positions where I can make slam: first, if West began with all five trumps (West will soon be forced to ruff and be endplayed in trumps), and second if East began with the singleton ten (it will drop).

I ruff the heart with the ace of spades (West underruffing) and exit with my club, and West has to lead into my J9 of trumps at trick twelve.

The full deal:

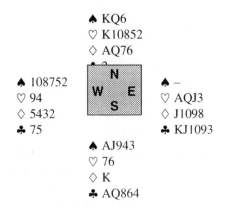

```
              ♠ KQ6
              ♡ K10852
              ◇ AQ76
                  ♣ ?
  ♠ 108752               ♠ —
  ♡ 94                   ♡ AQJ3
  ◇ 5432                 ◇ J1098
  ♣ 75                   ♣ KJ1093
              ♠ AJ943
              ♡ 76
              ◇ K
              ♣ AQ864
```

Post mortem

Had trumps really been 4-1 all along with West holding the ten, I may still have succeeded. If West makes the mistake of discarding his remaining diamond, the above endplay still works. His correct defence is to underruff when I ruff with the ace of spades. Then when I exit with a club, East can win the trick and play any card to enable West to make his ten of spades.

In addition, an expert East might have persuaded me to go wrong by playing the ace of hearts on the third round of the suit. I would surely have ruffed low, and an overruff and trump return would have beaten the slam.

The truth: The hand occurred in the Pairs Tournament at Deauville. In the large field only two declarers made twelve tricks.

Cutting the link

The bidding

Sitting South, fourth in hand at Love All, I pick up the following attractive collection:

♠ 64
♡ AKQ10543
◇ 2
♣ K76

Rather to my surprise, the first three players to speak all pass, and it is up to me. If partner were not a passed hand I would perhaps be rather good for a four heart opening bid, but the chances of slam being on when he could not open the bidding are minimal. Furthermore, a high-level opening bid is likely to keep East/West quiet. So I open four hearts and everybody passes.

The bidding has been:

West	North	East	South
Pass	Pass	Pass	4♡
All Pass			

The play

West leads the jack of clubs and dummy comes down with quite a suitable collection:

♠ AQJ9
♡ J
◇ 10873
♣ Q843

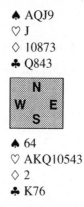

♠ 64
♡ AKQ10543
◇ 2
♣ K76

The early play seems straightforward. I play low on the club lead and win in hand with my king. I then play out hearts from the top. East follows to four rounds, while West follows once and then discards two spades and a diamond.

The problem is how to play the black suits. Obviously everything will be fine if the spade finesse is right, but West's two spade discards make that look a little unlikely. Suppose I start by taking the spade finesse. If it is wrong East will put West in with a diamond and now a club through dummy's king will mean one down.

Perhaps it is better to play a club first. Suppose I play a club and duck. If East's ace is doubleton there will be no problem, but if West's ten wins that trick, then a spade through dummy's tenace will spell defeat. It is no better if I cover the ten of clubs with the queen. East will put West in with a diamond and again a spade through dummy will beat me.

I am beginning to see the light. Both these successful defences depended on one opponent being able to reach the other's hand in diamonds. I think I shall play a diamond myself first.

West wins the diamond with the queen, as is surely best for the defence. But he can no longer harm me. If he plays a spade I finesse and East has no good play. I can eventually discard a club on dummy's spades. If he plays the ten of clubs I must be careful to cover. Again, East can do me no harm and I can establish the eight of clubs for a spade discard.

The full deal:

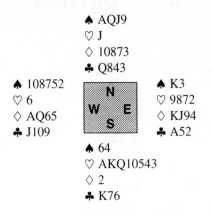

♠ AQJ9
♥ J
♦ 10873
♣ Q843

♠ 108752
♥ 6
♦ AQ65
♣ J109

♠ K3
♥ 9872
♦ KJ94
♣ A52

♠ 64
♥ AKQ10543
♦ 2
♣ K76

Post mortem

Provided declarer plays a diamond after drawing trumps (a play known as a Scissors Coup because it cuts the communications between the two defenders' hands), there is no successful defence. Although this hand is not difficult, it has an elegant symmetry in the black suits and the correct play is easy to overlook.

The truth: This deal occurred in the 1997 Open European Championships. Because the boards were duplicated, it was played many times, but failed much more often than it succeeded.

Pushy partner

The bidding

In second seat I pick up an above-average hand:

♠ 106
♡ AQ9876
◇ A4
♣ QJ2

My right-hand opponent passes and I open one heart. Partner responds one spade and I rebid my hearts. Partner raises to three hearts and I like my hand enough to press on to game.

The bidding has been:

West	North	East	South
–	–	Pass	1♡
Pass	1♠	Pass	2♡
Pass	3♡	Pass	4♡
All Pass			

The play

West leads the ten of clubs and I see these hands:

♠ KQ83
♡ 52
◇ J83
♣ A763

```
    N
  W   E
    S
```

♠ 106
♡ AQ9876
◇ A4
♣ QJ2

Partner has not been backward in the bidding but that comes as no particular surprise. There is quite a bit of work to do.

I have little choice but to play low from dummy at trick one. East plays the eight and I win the queen. Maybe I can set up a spade for a diamond discard, so at trick two I lead a spade towards dummy. The queen of spades holds, and I now play a heart. East plays the king and I win the ace to play another spade. West takes his ace and exits with another spade (East having played the seven on the first round, now following with the four and five) which I take with the king, pitching my diamond.

The king of hearts may well not be singleton, as many defenders would play the king from a doubleton, particularly if they also held the ten or jack. However, if hearts are breaking I have made my contract, so I must assume they are not. I do not have enough trump entries to reduce my trumps to the same length as West's and go for a trump endplay, so I must hope that a straightforward endplay will work.

I cross to the ace of diamonds and play the nine of hearts. If East can win this with the ten or jack and play a fourth spade I do not mind because I can discard a club and East will not have another spade to play. In the event West wins with the ten of hearts, East showing out, and plays the queen of diamonds which I ruff.

It looks as if West's original distribution was 3-4-2-4, and if that is the case, I have him. I cash the queen of hearts and exit with another heart. West has no option but to play a club for me so I avoid a loser in that suit and bring home my game.

The full deal:

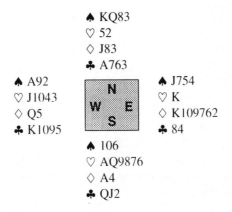

```
                  ♠ KQ83
                  ♡ 52
                  ◇ J83
                  ♣ A763
   ♠ A92                        ♠ J754
   ♡ J1043        N             ♡ K
   ◇ Q5        W     E          ◇ K109762
   ♣ K1095        S             ♣ 84
                  ♠ 106
                  ♡ AQ9876
                  ◇ A4
                  ♣ QJ2
```

Post mortem

The hand played itself once I realised that exiting with the nine of hearts might cause West a problem and couldn't do me any harm even if hearts broke. Of course if I play queen and another heart at that stage West will cash his other trump winner before exiting with his diamond and I will have to play clubs myself.

Note that West defended quite badly. When he won the ace of spades he should have exited with a diamond, not a spade. He can see that I cannot get to dummy to take my discard without destroying my club position.

The truth: The deal comes from the round-robin stage of the 2002 World Championship Power Rosenblum teams. England's Justin Hackett made his game by the play decribed above and his team went on to qualify for the knock-out stages where they reached the last 16.

Discovery play

The bidding

First in hand at Game All my partner, North, opens one club, East passes and I am looking at:

♠ A97
♡ 86
◇ AJ10973
♣ 95

I bid one diamond and partner rebids two no-trumps. Well, I guess I could raise straight to game but I rather like my hand and do not want to give up on chances of slam. Accordingly, I rebid three diamonds which my partner and I have agreed is forcing. Partner raises to four diamonds and I start to have cold feet. Perhaps I have been too pushy. I am not going to cue-bid my ace of spades. I shall simply settle for game. I have made my slam try and partner can always bid on if he is super-suitable.

The bidding has been:

West	North	East	South
–	1♣	Pass	1◇
Pass	2NT	Pass	3◇
Pass	4◇	Pass	5◇
All Pass			

The play

West leads the jack of spades and this is what I can see.

♠ K82
♡ A104
◇ K84
♣ AK64

♠ A97
♡ 86
◇ AJ10973
♣ 95

Oh dear, I guess I should have simply raised to three no-trumps. Still, it looks as if all I need to do is find the queen of diamonds. I think I am prepared to take some chances in the side-suits rather than simply guess diamonds at the start. After all, both opponents had a chance to overcall on the first round so it doesn't sound as if there is any wild distribution about.

I win the ace of spades in hand, and play dummy's top clubs and ruff a club (with the seven). Everyone follows. Now I am well placed. I will cross to the ace of hearts and play a fourth club. If East follows I will discard my heart loser. As it is, East throws a heart, so I ruff low, and exit with a heart.

West wins with the queen and plays another spade. I win my king in dummy and ruff a heart (with the nine). This is the position:

♠ 8
♡ –
◇ K84
♣ –

♠ 9
♡ –
◇ AJ10
♣ –

All I need to do is exit with a spade; whatever the defenders do gives me my contract.

The full deal:

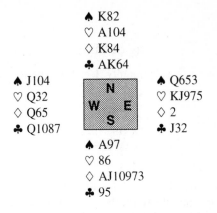

```
                    ♠ K82
                    ♡ A104
                    ◇ K84
                    ♣ AK64
   ♠ J104              N           ♠ Q653
   ♡ Q32                           ♡ KJ975
   ◇ Q65          W       E        ◇ 2
   ♣ Q1087            S            ♣ J32
                    ♠ A97
                    ♡ 86
                    ◇ AJ10973
                    ♣ 95
```

Post mortem

Obviously there were slight risks of being overruffed at any stage but that required West to have the queen of diamonds and to have two cards or fewer in either hearts or clubs. If that were the case then he probably had Qxx(x) in diamonds, which I would not have played for had I drawn trumps immediately.

The truth: No, I cannot claim credit for this, but it was played correctly at the table – by the great Giorgio Belladonna himself.

Entries and exits

The bidding

In fourth seat at adverse vulnerability, I pick up the following attractive collection:

♠ AQJ83
♡ A4
◇ AKQ842
♣ –

In this day and age, with this sort of distribution in fourth seat, particularly with the opponents non-vulnerable, there is little point in deciding what I should open as it is highly unlikely that I shall be allowed a free run.

Sure enough, West starts the ball rolling with a pre-emptive three hearts which is passed round to me.

When I started playing the game, the normal action on this type of hand was a four heart cue-bid, but times have changed. I have been persuaded of the futility of having a natural four of a minor overcall, so now I play that a bid of four of a minor is forcing, showing a two-suiter with the bid minor and spades. Thus a four heart cue-bid would show the minors, leaving four no-trumps as Blackwood (in the old days four no-trumps would have been for the minors). Non Leaping Michaels, I believe it is called.

So I settle for four diamonds, slightly anxiously as I would not like partner to take it into his head to pass.

Partner makes the rather surprising bid of five clubs. It is not clear exactly what that means, but it sounds as if he has something, so I decide to have a pot at six diamonds.

The bidding has been:

West	North	East	South
3♡	Pass	Pass	4◇
Pass	5♣	Pass	6◇
All Pass			

The play

West leads the king of hearts and this is what I can see:

♠ 62
♡ 73
◇ 109
♣ AKQ7642

```
      N
   W     E
      S
```

♠ AQJ83
♡ A4
◇ AKQ842
♣ –

Now I see what his five club bid was all about. I can't really find it in me to criticise him. Still, I will be in for my own share of criticism if I can't find a way to land this slam. Prospects don't look too good.

Superficially, the only hope seems to be to find someone with the singleton jack of diamonds. Then I can get to dummy, throw some losers on the top clubs and take a spade finesse... Even then it's not cold. There must be something better.

Suppose I just exit with a heart. Now East or West will have to do something. It looks fine if West is on lead and even if East wins the heart I should be reasonably well placed if he has both the king of spades and jack of diamonds.

So I win the ace of hearts, East playing the six, and exit with a heart. East wins the jack and exits with a low spade. I play the queen which holds. Now the ace of spades and a spade ruff in the dummy; they break 3-3. All I need now is to bring in the trumps for no loser. Assuming hearts were 7-2 (no certainty at this vulnerability), then I know ten of West's cards and only five of East's. Although some of the lay-outs are irrelevant, it is much more likely that the jack of diamonds is with East rather than West. So I play the ten of diamonds from dummy and let it run. When West plays low, I ruff a club back to hand, draw the remaining trumps and claim my slam.

The full deal:

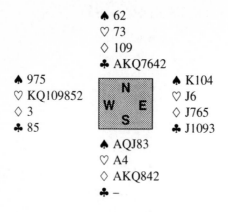

```
                    ♠ 62
                    ♡ 73
                    ◇ 109
                    ♣ AKQ7642
    ♠ 975                           ♠ K104
    ♡ KQ109852       N              ♡ J6
    ◇ 3          W       E          ◇ J765
    ♣ 85             S              ♣ J1093
                    ♠ AQJ83
                    ♡ A4
                    ◇ AKQ842
                    ♣ –
```

Post mortem

It was slightly strange of East to play a spade when he won the jack of hearts. A diamond switch looks more normal. I would still succeed, of course, as I would run the diamond. Now whether I play for clubs to break by cashing three winners in that suit before taking a spade finesse, or play for spades to break by taking an immediate spade finesse and ruffing a spade in the dummy, I must make my contract.

Can you see how the defenders could have triumphed. West needed to win the second heart and play a third round of the suit. I ruff in the dummy and East refuses to overruff. (If he overruffs, so do I. Then I cross to dummy's remaining trump – drawing West's in the process – and play three rounds of clubs pitching spades before taking a spade finesse for my contract). Now I don't have the entries to finesse in both spades and diamonds. I think we can forgive West for not finding that defence.

The truth: In real life, I would like to thank Malcolm Copley, a *BRIDGE Magazine* reader, for sending me the hand.

Working it out

The bidding

I pick up the following cards in third position, vulnerable against not:

♠ 64
♡ AKJ95
◇ A43
♣ A43

After two passes, I open one heart. Partner responds one spade and I rebid one no-trump, showing 15–17 points. Partner bids two clubs, which we play as checkback, asking if I have five hearts or three spades. I bid two hearts and partner bids two spades. In our methods this is forcing for one round and shows a decent five-card spade suit. Although I do not have a fitting honour in spades, I like my strong heart suit and my good controls, so I close the auction with a jump to three no-trumps.

The bidding has been:

West	North	East	South
–	Pass	Pass	1♡
Pass	1♠	Pass	1NT
Pass	2♣	Pass	2♡
Pass	2♠	Pass	3NT
All Pass			

The play

West leads the five of diamonds and this is what I can see:

♠ AJ1097
♡ 87
◇ K98
♣ 972

♠ 64
♡ AKJ95
◇ A43
♣ A43

Partner has nothing to spare and it looks as if I shall need some luck in the major suits if I am to succeed.

I play the eight of diamonds from dummy at trick one and East plays the queen. This suit combination is one where it is often right to duck, but here I do not want to risk a club switch. So I win my ace of diamonds and play a spade to dummy's jack and East's queen. East continues with the ten of diamonds and now I do duck, West following with the two. East switches to the king of clubs. I duck this as well, win the queen of clubs continuation and play a spade to dummy's ten, which holds. If spades break 3-3, I am home so I cash the ace of spades but, disappointingly, East discards a club. This is the position:

♠ 97
♡ 87
◇ K
♣ 9

♠ —
♡ AKJ95
◇ 4
♣ —

Perhaps I should turn my attention to hearts. If that suit comes in then I will have nine tricks (ten, actually). But, wait a moment. Surely West has five diamonds – that is what his carding in the suit seems to suggest, along with East's switch after the ten held. I know he has four spades and two clubs. So the heart suit cannot come in. I will be in a better position if I establish another spade trick, so I continue with the nine of spades.

West wins his king as East discards a club, and plays another diamond. I win in dummy, East throwing a heart, and cash my long spade, East pitching another heart and West a diamond. Now I know that East has a winning club left, so he can't have Qxx in hearts. And West has a winning diamond. There is no point finessing, so I play my hearts from the top and West's queen comes tumbling down.

The full deal:

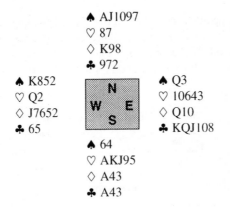

```
                ♠ AJ1097
                ♡ 87
                ◇ K98
                ♣ 972
 ♠ K852                        ♠ Q3
 ♡ Q2          N              ♡ 10643
 ◇ J7652    W     E           ◇ Q10
 ♣ 65          S              ♣ KQJ108
                ♠ 64
                ♡ AKJ95
                ◇ A43
                ♣ A43
```

Post mortem

This is an excellent example of how an expert plays a hand. Each step was calculated perfectly: winning the first diamond, ducking the second, ducking the club switch, realising the heart suit could not come in for four tricks (unless someone had an extremely unlikely queen-ten doubleton), and finally working out that it could not be right to take the heart finesse.

The truth: Well played! But not by me, it was Germany's Sabine Auken.

Shortening my trumps

The bidding

In fourth seat as South I pick up a good distributional hand with East/West only vulnerable:

♠ KJ98432
♡ 8
◇ AK62
♣ 4

My left-hand opponent starts the ball rolling by opening three clubs, which is passed round to me. I have a choice between three spades and four spades. I need so little (in the right places) that I decide on four spades. This goes round to East who doubles, and I await the dummy with some concern.

The bidding has been:

West	North	East	South
3♣	Pass	Pass	4♠
Pass	Pass	Dble	All Pass

The play

West leads the king of clubs and partner puts down his dummy:

♠ 65
♡ K9742
◇ J5
♣ AJ85

♠ KJ98432
♡ 8
◇ AK62
♣ 4

It doesn't look good. Spades are sure to break badly and if I ruff diamonds in dummy how will I avoid losing three spades and a heart? Perhaps I can make my trumps by ruffing, and endplay East in trumps at the end. For this type of play, strangely enough, the worse the spade break the better my chances.

I win the ace of clubs and ruff a club as East throws a heart. I cash the ace and king of diamonds and ruff a diamond, everyone following. I ruff another club as East throws yet another heart. I have made six tricks and need East to have started with four diamonds. I'm hoping the position is:

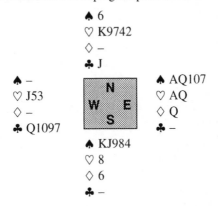

```
                    ♠ 6
                    ♡ K9742
                    ◇ -
                    ♣ J
  ♠ -                           ♠ AQ107
  ♡ J53          N              ♡ AQ
  ◇ -         W     E           ◇ Q
  ♣ Q1097        S              ♣ -
                    ♠ KJ984
                    ♡ 8
                    ◇ 6
                    ♣ -
```

If the spades are 4-0, I am going to make my contract. I ruff the diamond in dummy and another club in hand bringing my total to eight tricks and I still have the KJ98 of spades left. I lead my heart which East wins and I can either ruff the return or, if he plays a spade, finesse my jack. I then exit with a spade and must come to another trump trick.

The full deal:

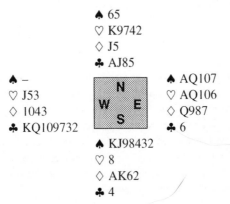

```
                    ♠ 65
                    ♡ K9742
                    ◇ J5
                    ♣ AJ85
  ♠ -                           ♠ AQ107
  ♡ J53          N              ♡ AQ106
  ◇ 1043       W     E          ◇ Q987
  ♣ KQ109732     S              ♣ 6
                    ♠ KJ98432
                    ♡ 8
                    ◇ AK62
                    ♣ 4
```

Post mortem

This was a hand on which a double advertised the bad breaks and helped declarer to choose a successful line, though a bad spade break was likely after West's opening bid in any event.

But wait, East should have been discarding diamonds. If he throws a diamond on either of the two occasions that declarer plays a low club from the dummy, he must make three tricks to go with his ace of hearts.

The truth: This hand was from the final of the 2002 World Mixed Pairs Championship. Several players made the contract when doubled. When the contract was not doubled there was a chance of taking one diamond ruff and playing a spade to the king hoping for a 2-2 split. However, this requires West to be 2-2-3-6, for with 2-1-3-7 he would probably have led his singleton heart. If declarer had ruffed a club at trick two he would have known that West had seven clubs and three diamonds so that a 2-2 spade division was highly unlikely. Sadly, my partner overlooked the necessity of ruffing a club at trick two and had to go one down.

No need to guess

The bidding

Sitting South at Love All, playing matchpointed pairs, I pick up the following:

♠ A103
♡ Q532
◊ A
♣ 108652

East is the dealer, and opens the bidding with two diamonds. This is alerted, and when I enquire I am told that it shows a weak two in diamonds, say 5–10 points and a six-card suit.

I do not really have enough to bid, but I am the one with the short diamonds. I can think of many decent hands partner could hold where he is stuck for a bid because he has diamond length. Anyway, I am not vulnerable so may not score badly even if I go down in the contract I eventually reach. So I double for take-out.

West raises to three diamonds which partner doubles. This is a responsive double. According to our agreement it shows both or neither major. Here it is likely to be both, so I bid three hearts, which partner raises to four.

The bidding has been:

West	North	East	South
—	—	2◊	Dble
3◊	Dble	Pass	3♡
Pass	4♡	All Pass	

The play

West leads the two of diamonds and this is what I can see:

♠ KJ95
♡ J974
◇ 107
♣ AQJ

```
      N
   W     E
      S
```

♠ A103
♡ Q532
◇ A
♣ 108652

Even though we are short of high-card values and would surely not have bid game if left to our own devices, I am happy with the final contract. I have only two top losers and there is plenty of scope to develop ten tricks. If West has the king of clubs I should be OK, and if not I will have to guess who has the queen of spades.

There seems no reason to postpone playing trumps as I have sufficient entries and control to play on the black suits later when I have more information to go on. So at trick two I play a low heart towards the dummy. West plays the king and East follows with the six. West now switches to the three of clubs.

Well, this could be a singleton but I doubt it. If West had a singleton club he might have led it at trick one. It is more likely that East has the club shortage. If West is hoping to give his partner a club ruff, then presumably he started with ace-king doubleton of hearts (if he had Kx he would/should have let his partner win the first trump in order for West to have an entry on the second round, while if West began with AKx of trumps he would know that partner would have no trumps left when a second club was played).

If I play a second trump now, West will win his ace and give East a club ruff. East will get off lead with a diamond and I will need to guess who has the queen of spades. Or, hang on a minute … maybe I can do better.

If the lay-out is as I think it is, I can make sure East is endplayed after he has ruffed the club. What I must do is ruff a diamond before playing a second round of trumps. Then he will have to open up spades or give me a ruff and discard.

So, on West's club switch I finesse successfully. Then I ruff a diamond and play a second trump. West wins the ace and plays a second club which East ruffs. East now thinks for a while before exiting with a third round of diamonds.

Surely I have a complete count of the hand now. East started with three hearts, presumably six diamonds, and one club. Spades must be 3-3. So I ruff the diamond in dummy while pitching a spade from my hand. Now the ace and king of spades and a spade ruff bring down West's Qxx, and dummy is high.

The full deal:

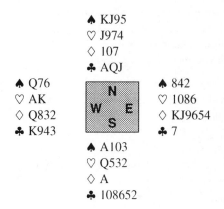

```
              ♠ KJ95
              ♡ J974
              ◇ 107
              ♣ AQJ
  ♠ Q76                      ♠ 842
  ♡ AK          N           ♡ 1086
  ◇ Q832    W       E       ◇ KJ9654
  ♣ K943        S           ♣ 7
              ♠ A103
              ♡ Q532
              ◇ A
              ♣ 108652
```

Post mortem

On this particular lay-out dummy's and East's spades were such that East could tell that there was no future in playing a spade, hence his decision to give the ruff and discard. In either event declarer cannot fail.

The truth: I was declarer on this deal at a Young Chelsea duplicate. In the event I overlooked the necessity of ruffing a diamond, so had to guess the spade position to make my game. I guessed right so I was quite happy. It was only afterwards that I realised there was a better line of play.

Squeezed in trumps

The bidding

First in hand at adverse vulnerability, I pick up:

♠ AQ4
♡ AKJ
◇ QJ7
♣ K853

An easy choice to start with: two no-trumps. Partner responds three clubs, Stayman, and I bid three diamonds, denying a four-card major. Partner proceeds with four diamonds, a natural slam try. I co-operate with a four heart cue-bid and partner bids four spades.

Maybe I should sign off now, but I do have a club control which will be protected as I will be declarer in diamonds, so I take the aggressive course and bid six diamonds.

The bidding has been:

West	North	East	South
–	–	–	2NT
Pass	3♣	Pass	3◇
Pass	4◇	Pass	4♡
Pass	4♠	Pass	6◇
All Pass			

The play

West leads the three of diamonds and this is what I can see:

♠ K52
♡ 9853
◇ AK864
♣ J

♠ AQ4
♡ AKJ
◇ QJ7
♣ K853

I was expecting (and hoping for) a club lead, and West's failure to oblige probably means that he has the ace.

Partner has got more or less what he promised and the fact that the slam is far from certain is my fault, not his. I will need the heart finesse, along with another trick which will either come from a 3-3 heart break or something good happening in clubs.

I play the king of diamonds from the dummy and try the jack of clubs. One of my hopes is that East will not cover when he has the queen. This time East does indeed play low on the club, but when I play low West wins with the queen and plays a second trump. I run this round to my hand, East showing out.

I was intending to ruff two clubs in dummy, hoping to bring down the ace, but the 4-1 trump split means I cannot afford to do this or West will have more trumps than I do. Still, one ruff looks safe, so I ruff a club and it is time to test the hearts. I play a heart to my jack which holds and continue with the ace. On this trick East plays the queen. I pause to consider. Obviously this could be a false-card but I can see that I have other chances if West began life with a 2-4-4-3 distribution. East is not a strong player and I am inclined to take the queen of hearts at face value.

I ruff another club and West's ace comes tumbling down. Now I play the king of spades and a spade to my ace. This is the position:

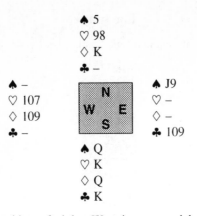

♠ 5
♡ 98
◇ K
♣ –

♠ –   ♠ J9
♡ 107   ♡ –
◇ 109   ◇ –
♣ –   ♣ 109

♠ Q
♡ K
◇ Q
♣ K

When I play the king of clubs, West is squeezed between trumps and hearts. If he plays a trump, I overruff, play a heart to my king, draw his trump and make my queen of spades at trick thirteen. If he discards a heart, I cash the king of hearts and make the last two tricks on a high cross-ruff

The full deal:

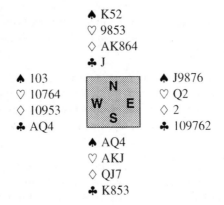

♠ K52
♡ 9853
◇ AK864
♣ J

♠ 103   ♠ J9876
♡ 10764   ♡ Q2
◇ 10953   ◇ 2
♣ AQ4   ♣ 109762

♠ AQ4
♡ AKJ
◇ QJ7
♣ K853

Post mortem

There was nothing the defenders could do. The key decision was whether to play for hearts 3-3 or for West to be 2-4-4-3.

The truth At the table in a league match, Raymond Brock, my partner in life as well as at the table, made his slam on the line given.

Dramatic reduction

The bidding

Sitting South, in second seat, vulnerable against not, I hold this interesting collection:

♠ A9865432
♡ AK
◇ J3
♣ J

After my right-hand opponent passes I have to decide what to open. I usually hate opening eight-card suits at the one level, as partner never expects such extreme distribution, but here, with such poor suit quality and my strong doubleton heart on the side, I can see no alternative to opening one spade.

My left-hand opponent bids two spades, which is alerted as being a Michaels cue-bid, showing hearts and a minor. My partner doubles, showing interest in taking a penalty, and my right-hand opponent passes. I could simply bid four spades but there seems no reason to rush things, so I pass for the time being and West bids three clubs, presumably showing five cards in the suit. Partner doubles and East passes. Well, it could be right to pass this but partner is probably doubling on the basis of my having some sort of semi-balanced hand, not an eight-card suit. I think that the odds favour me removing this double to four spades.

The bidding has been:

West	North	East	South
–	–	Pass	1 ♠
2 ♠	Dble	Pass	Pass
3 ♣	Dble	Pass	4 ♠
All Pass			

The play

West leads the ten of clubs and I can see:

♠ –
♡ 9863
◇ AKQ10
♣ AK854

♠ A9865432
♡ AK
◇ J3
♣ J

It looks as if we could have taken quite a penalty from three clubs. Still, four spades looks safe enough unless spades are 5-0. Actually, it is quite likely that they are 5-0, for West appears to have little enough for his Michaels cue-bid.

If trumps are 5-0, I may still be able to succeed, provided I can reduce my trumps to the same length as East's. To that end, I win the ace of clubs, cash the king of clubs, discarding a *heart* (East may have a singleton heart) and ruff a club (East pitching a diamond). I cash the ace of hearts, cross to the ace of diamonds and ruff a heart, now back to the king of diamonds and ruff another heart (East discarding another diamond).

This is the end position with the lead in my hand:

♠ –
♡ 9
◇ Q10
♣ 85

♠ A9865
♡ –
◇
♣ –

So far the only risk I have taken is to play West for at least two diamonds. I now exit with the nine of spades. If West has a spade I cannot lose more than three spade tricks, but in the event West shows out while East wins the nine of spades with the ten. He then plays the king of spades which I duck, followed by the queen of spades which I also duck. This leaves him with jack-seven while I have ace-eight, and he has to lead a spade for me at trick twelve.

The full deal:

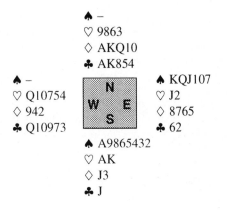

```
                    ♠ –
                    ♡ 9863
                    ◊ AKQ10
                    ♣ AK854
    ♠ –                          ♠ KQJ107
    ♡ Q10754        N            ♡ J2
    ◊ 942       W       E        ◊ 8765
    ♣ Q10973        S            ♣ 62
                    ♠ A9865432
                    ♡ AK
                    ◊ J3
                    ♣ J
```

Post mortem

Do you see where East went wrong? What he should have done was ruff high on two of the occasions that declarer plays hearts/clubs from dummy. In that way East also reduces his trumps so declarer cannot achieve his aim of ending up with the same length as East. Now East has plenty of exit cards and must make four trump tricks.

The truth A dramatic example of a trump reduction and endplay, but played by Wales's Tim Rees in a Crockford's match, not by me.

The three ducks

The bidding

Sitting East, in fourth seat vulnerable against not, I pick up an average sort of a hand:

♠ A106
♡ 9852
◇ Q63
♣ A105

My left-hand opponent, an aggressive player, opens a weak two spades, ostensibly showing 5–9 HCP with a six-card spade suit. Partner passes and North jumps straight to four spades, ending the auction.

The bidding has been:

West	North	East	South
–	–	–	2♠
Pass	4♠	All Pass	

The play

My partner leads the king of hearts, and this is what I can see:

♠ KQ2
♡ A4
◇ AJ4
♣ KJ842

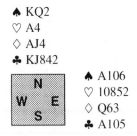

♠ A106
♡ 10852
◇ Q63
♣ A105

Dummy seems to have his bid. I shall have to hope that declarer is very weak. He is likely to be short of entries to his hand, so maybe we can capitalise on that.

Declarer wins the ace of hearts and plays the king of spades from the dummy. There seems to be no reason to win this trick, so I duck and declarer continues with the queen of spades. Assuming declarer has Jxxxxx in spades (or even Jxxxx), it will be best for me to duck this trick too, to prevent him getting to hand with the third round of the suit. I duck the second spade and partner discards the seven of hearts. Declarer now plays a low heart from the dummy. It would clearly be advantageous for me to win this trick, so I play the ten of hearts and declarer plays the nine while partner contributes the six. Since partner is marked with the queen and jack of hearts, I know that declarer must have started with a doubleton in the suit. I cash the ace of spades, partner pitching a diamond, and continue hearts.

Declarer ruffs in hand and plays the three of clubs. Partner plays the six and declarer plays dummy's jack. The six is the lowest outstanding club, so partner clearly began with Qxx. If I win this trick and play a fourth heart, declarer will ruff, play a club to the king and ruff a club establishing the suit. He will later be able to cross to dummy's ace of diamonds and pitch his diamond loser on dummy's club. So, I duck the jack of clubs. Declarer now plays a diamond to his king and another club. Partner plays the nine, declarer the king and I win the ace. Now I play a fourth round of hearts which declarer ruffs. He can no longer establish dummy's club suit and must fall back on the diamond finesse, so I win my queen of diamonds, our fourth defensive trick.

The full deal:

```
              ♠ KQ2
              ♡ A4
              ◇ AJ4
              ♣ KJ842
  ♠ 4           N         ♠ A106
  ♡ KQJ76                 ♡ 10852
  ◇ 10952     W   E       ◇ Q63
  ♣ Q96         S         ♣ A105
              ♠ J98753
              ♡ 93
              ◇ K87
              ♣ 73
```

Post mortem

Note that all three of East's ducks were necessary. If East wins the first spade he doesn't have anything good to play. The best he can do is cash the ten of hearts and play another spade. Declarer wins in hand and plays a club to the jack. But now, even if East ducks, declarer can play another club, win the return, cross to dummy with a spade, ruff a club, draw the last trump and cross to dummy's ace of diamonds to cash an established club to pitch my diamond loser. If West tries to attack dummy's diamond entry by winning the second round of hearts and switching to the ten of diamonds, declarer can later fall back on finessing him for the nine of diamonds.

The truth: This deal occurred in a multiple teams event at the Amersham bridge club. As far as I know every declarer was allowed to succeed.

Mistimed play

The bidding

Sitting South as dealer, vulnerable against not, I pick up the following:

♠ AJ83
♡ KQ7
◇ K42
♣ Q95

My partnership is using the weak no-trump, so, although there is a case for downgrading this barren 15-count and opening one no-trump anyway, I decide to take the more aggressive course and open one spade. Partner bids two diamonds and I rebid two no-trumps, showing 15–19 HCP. Partner, after a lot of thought, raises me to six no-trumps.

The bidding has been:

West	North	East	South
–	–	–	1♠
Pass	2◇	Pass	2NT
Pass	6NT	All Pass	

The play

West leads the three of hearts. Partner puts his hand down apologetically, telling me I should have no problem in making my slam and that he wanted to look for seven, etc, etc…' In my experience, that sort of comment usually precedes declarer going down in the contract he is actually in. And, indeed, when I see the dummy I observe that I have only eleven tricks on top.

♠ KQ6
♡ AJ4
◇ AQ108
♣ A87

♠ AJ83
♡ KQ7
◇ K42
♣ Q95

Well, I do have eleven tricks on top, with a twelfth readily available in diamonds should the suit break 3-3 or the jack drop. Failing that, I could either lead up to the queen of clubs, or else play for some sort of endplay.

My initial thoughts are to cash as many winners as I can before making my key play, but it looks as if I shall later play a low club towards my queen. If that loses I will take my chances in diamonds.

So, I win the ace of hearts in dummy (East playing the two) and play off four rounds of spades. All follow to the first two but West discards two clubs on the third and fourth spades. I discard a heart from the dummy. No hearts have been discarded so I can't afford to play off two more rounds of that suit. I next play the king and ace of diamonds. Rather disappointingly West discards another club on the second diamond.

This is the position, assuming from the play to trick one that West has four hearts to East's three:

♠ –
♡ J
◇ Q10
♣ A87

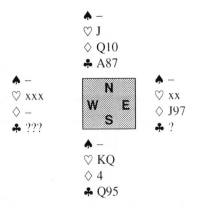

♠ –
♡ xxx
◇ –
♣ ???

♠ –
♡ xx
◇ J97
♣ ?

♠ –
♡ KQ
◇ 4
♣ Q95

Now my intended play of a low club towards the queen does not look so good. East is known to have started with nine cards in the pointed suits and probably had three hearts to West's four. In fact, East is showing every sign of having started life with a singleton club. If that is the case I can catch West in a curious sort of squeeze.

My next play is the key one: the queen of diamonds. West discards a heart. I am sure now that his original distribution was 2-4-1-6. So I cash two rounds of hearts, to which West and East both follow while I throw dummy's ten of diamonds. We are in a three-card end position:

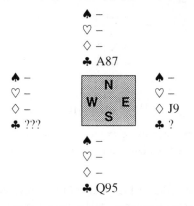

```
              ♠ –
              ♡ –
              ◇ –
              ♣ A87
 ♠ –                        ♠ –
 ♡ –          N             ♡ –
 ◇ –       W     E          ◇ J9
 ♣ ???        S             ♣ ?
              ♠ –
              ♡ –
              ◇ –
              ♣ Q95
```

If only I could see through the backs of the cards I would be cold now. As it is I have to guess whether West started with KJ10xxx or KJxxxx or K10xxxx or J10xxxx in clubs. As it happens I was watching his club spots carefully. So far he has thrown, in order, the two, the four and the six. Unless he is playing a deep game it looks as if East's singleton is the three. West looks to me like an honest sort of player.

I play a low club from hand and when West plays the ten, I duck. East does indeed follow with the three. West plays another club but I run it around to my queen and make my slam.

The full deal

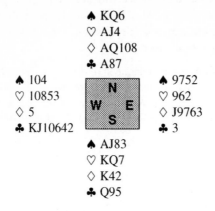

```
                    ♠ KQ6
                    ♡ AJ4
                    ◇ AQ108
                    ♣ A87
    ♠ 104                          ♠ 9752
    ♡ 10853            N           ♡ 962
    ◇ 5          W          E      ◇ J9763
    ♣ KJ10642          S           ♣ 3
                    ♠ AJ83
                    ♡ KQ7
                    ◇ K42
                    ♣ Q95
```

Post mortem

If West's clubs had initially been KJxxxx or K10xxxx, I would have had to play the queen of clubs from hand at trick eleven, pinning East's singleton honour.

I could still have succeeded if East had held the singleton nine of clubs, and I Q53. If West comes down to KJ10 clubs the play is as described above; alternatively, if he reduces to KJ6 of clubs, I can simply run the queen, setting up a second club trick by force.

Given the distribution of the deal, I mistimed it slightly. What I should have done was to play the ace and king of diamonds early. As soon as I discovered the 5-1 split, I would have been unhappy with the idea of playing East for the queen of clubs. Then when I played off my spades I could have discarded a diamond from dummy. This would have meant I could have cashed all my winners and been in dummy in the above three-card end position. That would have saved me a guess. I could simply have played the seven of clubs and run it if East played low; if East had played the jack or ten, I would have covered – either way West would have been endplayed.

The truth: This hand occurred in the US Blue Ribbon Pairs – an event I have never played in. The hand was played in the above fashion by Zia Mahmood and reported by Barry Rigal in *BRIDGE Magazine*.

Reading the distribution

The bidding

At Love All, first to speak, I hold the following excellent hand:

♠ QJ765
♡ AKJ5
◇ AQJ10
♣ –

I have high hopes. I open one spade and partner responds two clubs. It is not clear which red suit I should bid now, but as I still have fond hopes of a slam I want to investigate both fits; if I start with two diamonds it will be easier to find a heart fit than it will be to find a diamond fit if I start with two hearts.

Over two diamonds partner bids two hearts. Our agreement is that a raise of the fourth suit is natural if it can be, so this is what I bid now. Partner proceeds with four diamonds, setting the suit. I cue-bid four hearts and he bids four spades. It is beginning to sound as if he has long weak clubs with all his values in his short suits, in which case a grand slam is possible. I show my enthusiasm by cue-bidding above game, five hearts. Partner signs off in six diamonds which, rather to my surprise, East doubles.

The bidding has been:

West	North	East	South
–	–	–	1 ♠
Pass	2 ♣	Pass	2 ◇
Pass	2 ♡	Pass	3 ♡
Pass	4 ◇	Pass	4 ♡
Pass	4 ♠	Pass	5 ♡
Pass	6 ◇	Dble	All Pass

The play

West leads the queen of clubs and this is what I can see:

    ♠ K8
    ♡ 10
    ◇ 9864
    ♣ AK8753

    ♠ QJ765
    ♡ AKJ5
    ◇ AQJ10
    ♣ –

It seems as if partner has suffered from a rush of blood to the head! I don't know what was wrong with a simple raise of two diamonds to three. Instead, partner has forced to game which, facing my monster, has propelled us to slam and now it sounds as if the suits are breaking badly.

Still, the play's the thing! I play the ace of clubs from dummy at trick one, half expecting East to ruff it, but he follows with the ten and I throw a heart. I now take a diamond finesse, which holds and, to my relief, West follows. The time has come to play a spade. West plays the nine, dummy the king and East the ace. A diamond comes back and I finesse again as West shows out.

It is beginning to look very much as if East's distribution is 4-4-4-1. This is the position:

    ♠ 8
    ♡ 10
    ◇ 98
    ♣ K8753

    ♠ QJ76
    ♡ AKJ
    ◇ AQ
    ♣ –

My problem is that I need to ruff a spade *and* a heart in the dummy and still pick up East's trumps.

I cash my two top spades and ruff a spade – I was right about the distribution of that suit. Now I see what I must do. I cash my top hearts and ruff a heart. I am in dummy at trick eleven and all dummy has left are clubs. In hand are a winning spade and the ace and queen of diamonds. I play the king of clubs. If East ruffs, I overruff, draw his trump and claim; if he discards, I throw my winning spade and, with the lead in dummy, must make the last two tricks.

The full deal:

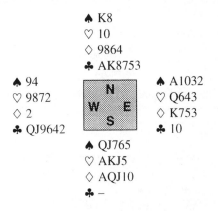

```
                ♠ K8
                ♡ 10
                ◇ 9864
                ♣ AK8753
  ♠ 94                        ♠ A1032
  ♡ 9872          N           ♡ Q643
  ◇ 2         W       E       ◇ K753
  ♣ QJ9642        S           ♣ 10
                ♠ QJ765
                ♡ AKJ5
                ◇ AQJ10
                ♣ –
```

Post mortem

At first sight it looks as if East was helpful to return a trump when in with the ace of spades. Say he returns a heart instead. Now I play off my two top hearts, ruff a heart, finesse in diamonds, play the queen and jack of spades and ruff a spade and I am in the same position as before.

It was nice of East to double, but in truth it did not really give the game away – it was the play of the hand that told me about the distribution, not the bidding.

The truth: This hand was shown me by my friend, Carole Mueller. She played the same way early on, but after East had played a second trump she cashed the ace and king of hearts discarding a spade from the dummy, and ruffed a spade. This avoided the possibility of East overruffing when he had the doubleton spade. Had the king of clubs stood up for a heart discard, she could have taken another trump finesse and claimed. However, when East ruffed the king of clubs she was one down.

Cavendish teams

The bidding

I am sitting South in the Cavendish Teams (an event where the teams are auctioned and the buyer of the winning team collects some hundreds of thousands of US dollars) in Las Vegas when I pick up, as dealer:

♠ 852
♡ K2
◇ AK96
♣ KQ63

With East/West silent throughout, I open one diamond, North responds one spade, I rebid one no-trump (15–17), and North raises to three no-trumps.

The bidding has been:

West	North	East	South
–	–	–	1◇
Pass	1♠	Pass	1NT
Pass	3NT	All Pass	

The play

West leads the six of hearts and dummy is tabled. This is what I can see:

♠ QJ109
♡ AJ5
◇ Q83
♣ 1094

```
      N
  W       E
      S
```

♠ 852
♡ K2
◇ AK96
♣ KQ63

On consulting their convention card I discover that my opponents lead fourth highest from honours and second highest from poor suits. The six of hearts is hard to read but I can preserve my options by playing low from dummy and winning with my king in hand. This gives East the chance to play the queen if he doesn't have a useful intermediate, a fairly forlorn hope in such a strong field, and indeed East plays the nine.

I can make nine tricks in a variety of ways. Two spades, two hearts, three diamonds and one club are guaranteed; the ninth may come from the heart finesse, a diamond break or a useful club position. However, first I have to knock out a few high cards in the black suits. I play a spade to dummy's nine which holds the trick, then a second spade which East wins with the king. He plays the seven clubs and my queen wins. Now I play my third spade to East's ace as West throws the three of hearts. East continues with the eight of clubs on which I play low as West wins with the jack.

So far so good. I have eight tricks on top and have lost three tricks. West exits with the eight of hearts and this is the moment of truth. I don't like to take a losing heart finesse when there are other options so I play the ace of hearts. This is the position:

♠ Q
♡ J
◇ Q83
♣ 10

```
    N
  W   E
    S
```

♠ –
♡ –
◇ AK96
♣ K6

When I cash the queen of spades, East follows as I throw a club and West a heart. I am really uncertain about the heart position. Did West start with four small or six to the queen? If the latter, then East will have the diamond length and if West has a doubleton ten or jack I may well be able to make four diamond tricks by finessing against East.

I play a diamond to the king and one back to the queen but it is East who drops the jack. I think West began with four small hearts and has none left now. I play a club which West wins and he has to lead into my ace-nine of diamonds to give me my ninth trick.

The full deal:

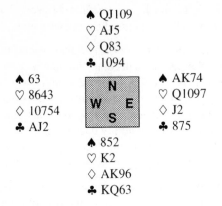

```
                    ♠ QJ109
                    ♡ AJ5
                    ◇ Q83
                    ♣ 1094
  ♠ 63                              ♠ AK74
  ♡ 8643            N               ♡ Q1097
  ◇ 10754        W     E            ◇ J2
  ♣ AJ2             S               ♣ 875
                    ♠ 852
                    ♡ K2
                    ◇ AK96
                    ♣ KQ63
```

Post mortem

Did you see where West went wrong? He should win the first club and continue hearts then, when East wins the second spade, he has two heart tricks to cash.

As West was a world champion, had there been an alternative I would not have played for a misdefence. But when the crucial decision was made (to exit with a club in the ending rather than play for diamonds to break), the only alternative explanation was that East had played the jack of diamonds on the second round from an original holding of J10xx, thus giving me a finesse position that was not rightfully mine – surely a less likely possibility.

The truth: In real life I didn't play in this year's prestigious Cavendish event but the successful declarer was French international star, Alain Levy.

It might have been...

The bidding

In third seat with East/West vulnerable I pick up a good hand as South:

♠ AQ106
♡ AKQ108
♢ K103
♣ 10

Partner passes and my right-hand opponent opens one club which I double. West passes and partner responds one diamond. East bids two clubs and I bid two hearts. Now, rather to my surprise, partner jumps to four hearts. I should probably pass this, but, viewing the hand through rosy-coloured spectacles, I decide to look for a slam by cue-bidding four spades. That is enough for partner to jump to slam.

The bidding has been:

West	North	East	South
–	Pass	1♣	Dble
Pass	1♢	2♣	2♡
Pass	4♡	Pass	4♠
Pass	6♡	All Pass	

The play

West leads the jack of clubs and this is what I can see:

♠ K4
♡ J93
◇ A984
♣ 8753

♠ AQ106
♡ AKQ108
◇ K103
♣ 10

West's jack of clubs wins trick one and he continues with another club to East's queen.

It does look as though I have been too aggressive. Partner could hardly have more and content himself with a simple one diamond bid, yet I have only ten top tricks. I can ruff a spade in dummy to bring my total to eleven and then hope that I can squeeze East in the minors.

Alternatively I can draw two trumps and play four rounds of spades, hoping that I have four spade winners and that no-one will ruff while I discard two of dummy's diamonds; then I can ruff a diamond in dummy. I don't like that line very much.

The other possibility is to play a dummy reversal, ruffing two more clubs in hand. That will give me eleven tricks and then perhaps I can squeeze West in diamonds and spades. I like this third line for there is the additional chance that the jack of spades may drop.

I ruff the queen of clubs in hand with the eight, cash the ace of hearts and play the ten of hearts to the jack. If hearts are 4-1 the dummy reversal will not work and I will have to go for one of the other lines. But here everyone follows so I can continue with my plan. I ruff a club with the king of hearts and cross to dummy with the ace of diamonds to ruff the last club with the queen of hearts. West has yet to discard and this is the position:

```
              ♠ K4
              ♡ 9
              ◇ 984
              ♣ –
♠ J972                        ♠ 853
♡ 7                           ♡ –
◇ J7          [W N E S]       ◇ Q
♣ –                           ♣ A2
              ♠ AQ106
              ♡ –
              ◇ K10
              ♣
```

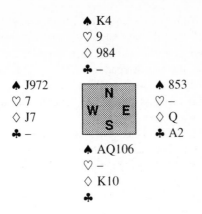

West does the best he can by underruffing. Now I cash the king of diamonds before crossing to the king of spades. When I cash dummy's master trump I throw the ten of diamonds but West can no longer delay the inevitable. If he throws a spade my hand will be high, while a discard of the jack of diamonds sets up dummy's nine and eight as winners.

The full deal:

```
              ♠ K4
              ♡ J93
              ◇ A984
              ♣ 8753
♠ J972                        ♠ 853
♡ 754         [W N E S]       ♡ 62
◇ J762                        ◇ Q5
♣ J9                          ♣ AKQ642
              ♠ AQ106
              ♡ AKQ108
              ◇ K103
              ♣ 10
```

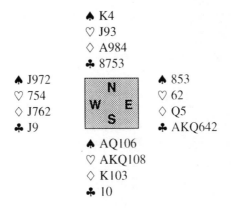

Post mortem

A dummy reversal nearly always requires the trumps to break and this should be tested as soon as possible whilst alternative lines are still available. Hence the early play of two rounds of trumps. Here if anyone was going to be short in hearts, it was surely going to be East. If East had shown out on the second round of trumps, I would have had to choose between the alternative two lines suggested above, though to some degree they can be combined. I would have continued with three rounds of spades, discarding a diamond from the dummy. If the jack of spades drops from East, I can now play the ten of spades pitching a diamond, and ruff a diamond in the dummy. If the ten of spades is not a master, I ruff it, ruff a club back to hand, draw trumps and play to squeeze East in the minors.

It was necessary for declarer to cash the king of diamonds before crossing to dummy in the end position above, otherwise the position would have been blocked and West could throw a diamond with impunity.

The truth Well no-one played it quite like that. The original hand, sent to me by Colin Jones, was as follows:

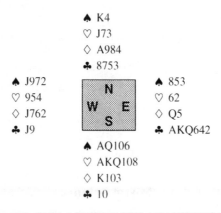

	♠ K4	
	♡ J73	
	◇ A984	
	♣ 8753	
♠ J972		♠ 853
♡ 954		♡ 62
◇ J762		◇ Q5
♣ J9		♣ AKQ642
	♠ AQ106	
	♡ AKQ108	
	◇ K103	
	♣ 10	

He asked what two spot cards could be interchanged so that the slam would make. He suggested the eight and seven of hearts. This would work but, in addition to all the good play described above, it also requires declarer to take a deep heart finesse at trick four: after running the second club high, he must cash a top heart and then play his seven to dummy's eight, before proceeding as above.

Stepping stone

The bidding

Sitting South, as the dealer at Love All, I pick up:

♠ J108
♡ QJ8
◊ K108
♣ A1065

With only 11 HCP and a 4-3-3-3 distribution, I suppose I should pass, but I am seduced by my array of tens. I open one no-trump. West bids two clubs which is alerted and, on enquiry, turns out to show both major suits. My partner doubles, and East bids two diamonds. I pass, as does West, and my partner bids two spades. I imagine he has a spade stopper but lacks a heart stopper (and maybe a diamond stopper too). Since I can help on both counts, I bid two no-trumps and he raises me to three.

The bidding has gone:

West	North	East	South
–	–	–	1NT
2♣	Dble	2◊	Pass
Pass	2♠	Pass	2NT
Pass	3NT	All Pass	

The play

West leads the ace of hearts, and partner puts down:

♠ AQ74
♡ 1063
◇ Q7
♣ KQ73

♠ J108
♡ QJ8
◇ K108
♣ A1065

At trick two West continues with the king and another heart, East discarding a low diamond on the third round.

West's play makes it obvious that he holds the ace of diamonds, but I should be able to get home with the aid of four spades (West surely has the king, and probably the nine too) and four clubs to go with the heart already in the bag. So I win the third heart in hand and play the jack of spades. When this holds I continue with the ten of spades which West covers with the king as East discards another diamond.

Ah, I am beginning to see a problem. Suppose I play clubs in normal fashion (i.e. the king, then the queen and then small to my hand in order to cater for Jxxx with East), and then I play the eight of spades: assuming West does not cover I cannot get back to dummy to cash the queen of spades.

Perhaps the solution is to take a second round finesse of the ten of clubs. That still caters for East having Jxxx, and will lose only if West has Jx. That will leave one of the top honours in dummy as an entry for the queen of spades. It would be unlucky to go down.

I play the king of clubs from the dummy and everyone follows, but now a further thought occurs to me. Of course, I do not need to take this risk in clubs. If I play clubs in normal fashion, West will have to find some discards. If he keeps only one spade I can overtake my eight with dummy's queen, while if he keeps two spades I can play the eight and then exit with a diamond and he will have to give dummy the queen of spades at trick thirteen.

So, I change my mind and continue with the queen of clubs – on which West's jack falls. I clearly had been about to make an embarrassing error. I continue with the rest of the suit and this is the position with West still to discard:

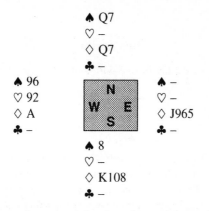

♠ Q7
♡ –
◊ Q7
♣ –

♠ 96   ♠ –
♡ 92   ♡ –
◊ A   ◊ J965
♣ –   ♣ –

♠ 8
♡ –
◊ K108
♣ –

If he throws a heart, I run the eight of spades, and then exit with a diamond. After cashing his last heart he has to give dummy the last trick – a stepping-stone squeeze.

The full deal:

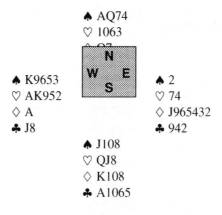

♠ AQ74
♡ 1063

♠ K9653   ♠ 2
♡ AK952   ♡ 74
◊ A   ◊ J965432
♣ J8   ♣ 942

♠ J108
♡ QJ8
◊ K108
♣ A1065

The truth: I have absolutely no idea! When I collect hands I always make a note of when and where they occurred and what the outcome was. But I must have been distracted when I recorded this one because I have no such details. It would be a pity to reject a hand for a book merely because of lack of provenance.

Three-three fit

The bidding

Sitting South playing rubber bridge with a 40 partscore, I pick up:

♠ K104
♥ 876
&diamonds; A94
♣ 9863

My left-hand opponent opens one club which partner doubles. One heart on my right, I pass and my left-hand opponent rebids two clubs which is passed around to me. It seems feeble to pass this out when we have a 40 partscore. I shall try an esoteric two spades. Surely I can't have a four-card suit or I would have bid on the previous round. For better or worse, my bid ends the auction.

The bidding has been:

West	North	East	South
1 ♣	Dble	1 ♥	Pass
2 ♣	Pass	Pass	2 ♠
All Pass			

The play

West leads the king of clubs and this is what I can see:

♠ AJ7
♥ J943
&diamonds; QJ102
♣ A5

	N	
W		E
	S	

♠ K104
♥ 876
&diamonds; A94
♣ 9863

I have been a bit too clever here. Although partner may have been able to work out that I have only three spades, it is not clear what I expected him to do with this piece of information. It hardly looked attractive for him to go gallivanting about at the three level in search of some other fit.

I win the ace of clubs and try the queen of diamonds. My spirits lift as it holds. I play a diamond to my nine, cash the ace of diamonds and exit with a club. West wins and cashes the ace and king of hearts before playing a third round of clubs. I ruff hopefully with the jack and again my luck is in – East discards a heart.

My trick total is now up to seven but it is hard to see where an eighth may come from. I try my winning diamond from the dummy. East ruffs and I discard my losing heart. East now tries the queen of hearts and I ruff with the king of spades as West discards a club. This is the position:

♠ A7
♡ J
♢ –
♣ –

♠ 104
♡ –
♢ –
♣ 9

All I can do is play my last club. West ruffs low. I discard my heart from the dummy and East starts to think, and think... Ah, now I realise that West must have Q65 and East 983.

If East allows his partner to win this trick, West will be endplayed. But if East overtakes with the eight of spades, all he can do is play another spade and if I play low from hand, West must play his queen to prevent my seven in dummy from scoring. My ten of spades will win trick thirteen.

This was the full deal:

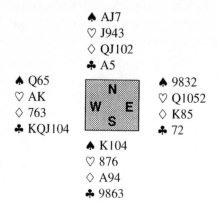

```
              ♠ AJ7
              ♡ J943
              ◇ QJ102
              ♣ A5
  ♠ Q65                    ♠ 9832
  ♡ AK          N          ♡ Q1052
  ◇ 763    W         E     ◇ K85
  ♣ KQJ104       S         ♣ 72
              ♠ K104
              ♡ 876
              ◇ A94
              ♣ 9863
```

Post mortem

East/West had too many trumps between them. West could have prevented the interesting end position by underruffing when I ruffed with the king of spades. Then on the next trick he would have followed to the club and if I had discarded from dummy East could have ruffed with his small trump.

Still, it was a very pretty ending and South's enterprise in the bidding was rewarded.

The truth: Not me, of course, but my regular partner, Margaret James, who can frequently be found in the £10 game at TGR's on a weekday afternoon.

En passant

The bidding

As South in fourth seat I pick up a fairly miserable collection:

♠ 10
♡ 109652
♢ K106
♣ Q976

My left-hand opponent, vulnerable against not, opens a weak two spades. My partner doubles and the next opponent passes. In our style I can bid an artificial two no-trumps and when partner bids the forced three clubs, remove it to three hearts in order to show a poor hand. Alternatively I can bid a direct three hearts which usually shows rather more points than I have, say, 8–10. However, East hasn't raised spades which makes it probable that partner has some spade length. If that is so he will have a good hand and my spade shortage will be useful. I choose to bid three hearts and not surprisingly partner raises to four hearts.

The bidding has been:

West	North	East	South
2♠	Dble	Pass	3♡
Pass	4♡	All Pass	

The play

West leads the four of clubs and partner puts down his dummy. This is what I can see:

♠ Q853
♡ KQ7
◇ AJ
♣ AK32

♠ 10
♡ 109652
◇ K106
♣ Q976

It looks as if I can expect two heart losers and one spade, but the lead looks ominously like a singleton so I may need to find the queen of diamonds, or perhaps the ace of hearts is with West.

I play the two of clubs from dummy and win my queen over East's ten. West must have a better lead than four to the jack so I am sure that the club is a singleton. I play the two of hearts to the eight, queen and three. I am short of entries to my hand but need to find the diamond queen for a club discard. Since it is more likely to be with East than West, I play the ace of diamonds and run the jack, which holds. I now play a spade from the table. East goes in with the king of spades, cashes the ace of hearts as West discards, and plays another heart so that I cannot ruff my fourth club in dummy. The position is:

♠ Q85
♡ –
◇ –
♣ AK3

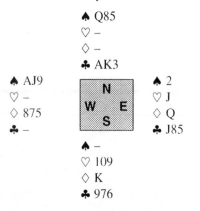

♠ AJ9
♡ –
◇ 875
♣ –

♠ 2
♡ J
◇ Q
♣ J85

♠ –
♡ 109
◇ K
♣ 976

The lead is in dummy and I have made five tricks: two hearts, two diamonds and one club. But the light has dawned and I can see my way home now. I ruff a spade, cash the king of diamonds and the ace and king of clubs in dummy. Finally, I lead a spade from dummy and, with East holding the jack of hearts and the jack of clubs whilst I have the ten of hearts and the nine of clubs, I must make the ten of hearts, en passant, as my tenth trick.

The full deal was:

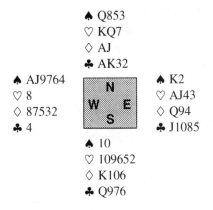

```
                   ♠ Q853
                   ♡ KQ7
                   ◇ AJ
                   ♣ AK32
   ♠ AJ9764                      ♠ K2
   ♡ 8            N              ♡ AJ43
   ◇ 87532   W         E         ◇ Q94
   ♣ 4            S              ♣ J1085
                   ♠ 10
                   ♡ 109652
                   ◇ K106
                   ♣ Q976
```

Post mortem

As is so often the case, the singleton club lead made it easier for declarer to find the winning line. On a trump lead it would seem more natural for declarer to ruff a diamond in the dummy and rely on making four club tricks.

The truth: The hand is from the quarter-finals of the 2002 Power Rosenblum World Teams Championships when team Lavazza of Italy crushed Kowalski of Poland. Versace for Italy played in three hearts and made four, whilst Szymanowski for Poland played in four hearts and made only three.

Surprising trump break

The bidding

Sitting South at Game All, I hear East on my right open three hearts. For once after a pre-empt I don't have much of a problem:

♠ A108753
♡ K87
◇ –
♣ AQ52

I bid three spades and am pleasantly surprised to hear partner cue-bid four hearts. If partner is interested in slam that's fine by me, so I make a return cue-bid of five clubs and partner closes proceedings with a leap to six spades.

The bidding has been:

West	North	East	South
–	–	3♡	3♠
Pass	4♡	Pass	5♣
Pass	6♠	All Pass	

The play

West leads the ace of diamonds and this is what I can see:

♠ KQJ62
♡ –
◇ K1064
♣ 10964

♠ A108753
♡ K87
◇ –
♣ AQ52

My first impressions are favourable, particularly after this opening lead. It looks as if I have six trump tricks in hand and three in dummy along with the king of diamonds and the ace of clubs. Hopefully I will eventually be able to endplay West by running the ten of clubs to his hand, forcing him either to play a club or to give me a ruff and discard. Can I foresee any problems?

If I am going to ruff three hearts in the dummy and then hope for an endplay, I will be fine if the trumps break 1-1. But can I do anything if they are 2-0?

It is hard to see how the end position might develop but it is important that I keep as many options open as possible. If it looks as if the club endplay won't work then I may have to try something else. I ruff trick one in hand, ruff a heart in dummy and cross back to hand with a trump.

Rather surprisingly, *West* shows out. Now the elimination play I had planned is unlikely to work because it looks likely that clubs are 4-1. If I draw both East's trumps as well as eliminating both red suits I will run out of trumps, while if I don't draw his trumps, when West gets in with his club honour he can give East a club ruff.

There seems nothing better to do than ruff another heart in the dummy, come back to hand with a trump, ruff a heart and ruff a diamond back to hand. This is the position:

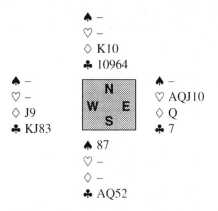

♠ –
♡ –
◇ K10
♣ 10964

♠ –   ♠ –
♡ –   ♡ AQJ10
◇ J9   ◇ Q
♣ KJ83   ♣ 7

♠ 87
♡ –
◇ –
♣ AQ52

I cash one spade and West discards a club (as does dummy), but what does he discard on the last spade? If he discards a second club, it is a simple matter for me to discard a diamond from the dummy and exit with the queen of clubs. Now all my clubs in hand are good.

His alternative is to discard a diamond. Now I discard a second club from
dummy and exit with a low club. West can win his jack but then has the
unenviable choice of either a diamond, giving dummy two tricks, or
another club which gives me the rest of the suit.

The full deal:

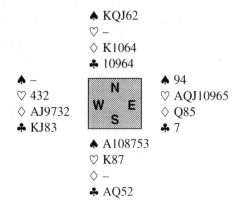

♠ KQJ62
♥ –
♦ K1064
♣ 10964

♠ –
♥ 432
♦ AJ9732
♣ KJ83

♠ 94
♥ AQJ10965
♦ Q85
♣ 7

♠ A108753
♥ K87
♦ –
♣ AQ52

Post mortem

Note that it is important for declarer to discover the trump position before
it is too late. If declarer embarks on the cross-ruff too early he will find that
he has ruffed all dummy's losing diamonds (i.e. one of his potential
winners) before he discovers the unexpected trump break.

The truth: This hand occurred in the quarter-finals of the 2001 Bermuda Bowl and
Venice Cup. I, along with every other declarer in the field who got the ace of
diamonds lead, fell into the trap of ruffing diamonds too early and thus failed to
make my slam.

Not the best fit

The bidding

Sitting South, first in hand, vulnerable against not, I pick up:

- ♠ AJ1095
- ♡ A92
- ◇ 4
- ♣ A862

On this occasion, I am playing a five-card major system. I open one spade, my left-hand opponent passes and partner responds one no-trump. In our system this can be up to a good 10 HCP, but even so there is unlikely to be a game on, so I content myself with a simple two clubs. Slightly surprisingly, West now enters the fray with two diamonds, and even more surprisingly, partner sallies forth with *three* spades. This is a very unusual call because he would usually raise me directly with three-card support. He must have a doubleton spade honour and a good club fit with me. I like my aces and my trump intermediates, so I press on to four spades.

The bidding has been:

West	North	East	South
–	–	–	1 ♠
Pass	1NT	Pass	2 ♣
2 ◇	3 ♠	Pass	4 ♠
All Pass			

The play

West leads the ace of diamonds and partner puts down his hand:

♠ K4
♡ J10753
◇ Q106
♣ KJ3

♠ AJ1095
♡ A92
◇ 4
♣ A862

Oh dear, it looks as if we have missed our best spot. Once partner chose to respond one no-trump to start with (a decision for which I have a lot of sympathy) it was difficult for us to find our heart fit. Still, four spades is the contract I must try to make.

At trick two West continues with the king of diamonds. This defence, combined with West's slightly unusual bidding, combine to make me think that it is West who has the spade length. Accordingly, I ruff the king of diamonds and play the nine of spades, running it when West plays low. The nine of spades holds and now I cross to dummy's king of spades and play a heart to my nine and West's queen.

West now exits with the nine of clubs. I win in dummy with the king and play dummy's jack of hearts, which holds the trick. I pause to take stock.

West's distribution is surely 4-2-5-2. If I play another heart now, West will ruff and play a club. I will have lost three tricks and will still have to lose a club to East. But if I am right about West's distribution, I can make him give me an entry to dummy. I play a low club off the dummy. East plays the ten and I win the ace. I now play ace and another spade and West has to win and give me entry to dummy with a diamond.

The full deal:

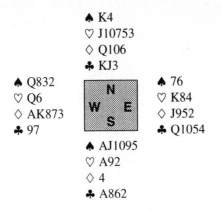

♠ K4
♥ J10753
&diamonds; Q106
♣ KJ3

♠ Q832
♥ Q6
&diamonds; AK873
♣ 97

♠ 76
♥ K84
&diamonds; J952
♣ Q1054

♠ AJ1095
♥ A92
&diamonds; 4
♣ A862

Post mortem

It looks as if West may have been able to defeat me by throwing his queen of spades under my ace. But that doesn't work either. I draw West's other trump and play a club to dummy's jack. If East ducks, dummy is high, while if he wins he has to play either a diamond giving me the dummy, or a club giving me an extra club trick in hand.

The truth: This hand was played as outlined above in the 2000 Sicilian Open Teams tournament, but declarer was not me but former Swedish and English international, Gunnar Hallberg. In the other room their Italian opponents managed to find the better fit and played in four hearts, but declarer lost his way in the play and went one down. The deal was originally reported by Patrick Jourdain.

Escape from the web

The bidding

Sitting South, in third seat vulnerable against not, I pick up:

♠ KJ9
♡ K1073
◊ KQ2
♣ 743

Partner opens one club and, and after East passes, I respond one heart. Partner raises to two hearts. He may not have four hearts for his raise so I bid three no-trumps, confident that he will put me back to four hearts if he has four-card support. However, he passes, ending the auction.

The bidding has been:

West	North	East	South
–	1♣	Pass	1♡
Pass	2♡	Pass	3NT
All Pass			

The play

My left-hand opponent leads the six of spades, and this is what I can see:

♠ 5
♡ AQ4
◊ 9753
♣ AK1082

```
    N
W       E
    S
```

♠ KJ9
♡ K1073
◊ KQ2
♣ 743

Despite dummy having sound values I have some work to do. However, it is hard to make a plan until I have a better idea of the spade position. I play low from dummy and East plays the queen, which I win with the king.

It looks as though I need to establish the clubs, but if East gains the lead and West has the ace and ten of spades I am in danger of losing four spade tricks. Maybe I can duck a club to West. If he has the queen, provided I lead up to dummy's holding twice, I can keep East off lead – by ducking if West plays the queen, or rising with one of dummy's honours otherwise. I play the four of clubs and West follows with the jack.

I can see no advantage in ducking this. If he has played the jack from jack doubleton, East will overtake the queen anyway. If by some miracle West has queen-jack doubleton I have nine tricks on top now, while if I play a diamond immediately and East has the ace and West the ace and ten of spades I will go down. It seems to cost little to play for this small possibility, so at trick three I cash the king of clubs. Much as expected, West shows out, discarding a diamond.

It will take too long to set up the fifth club so I must turn my attention to the red suits. I play a diamond to my king. West wins with the ace and exits with the two of spades to East's ten and my jack. This is the position:

```
              ♠ –
              ♡ AQ4
              ◇ 975
              ♣ 1082
            ┌─────────┐
            │    N    │
            │ W     E │
            │    S    │
            └─────────┘
              ♠ 9
              ♡ K1073
              ◇ Q2
              ♣ 7
```

I have made two clubs and two spades, and have one diamond and three hearts – eight in total. If hearts are 3-3 or the jack drops I have my nine tricks. If hearts are 4-2 with West having the jack perhaps I have the chance of an endplay.

I cash the ace and queen of hearts but the jack doesn't drop. It is time to consider West's distribution, but first I cash the queen of diamonds, on which West follows with the ten. I know that West started with one club and five spades (he led the six and then played the two; he would probably have overcalled one spade with a six-card suit and two aces). He has followed to two hearts and two diamonds and thrown a diamond. He has two unknown cards. Does he have one heart and one diamond or two hearts (I do not think he began with a five-card diamond suit)? I think the latter is more likely. If he began with four diamonds, his hand would have been ♠Axxxx ♡xxx ◊AJ10x ♣J and he might have bid one spade over my one heart.

So I exit with my spade and, after West cashes two more spades, he has to play a heart and I make two more heart tricks for my contract.

The full deal:

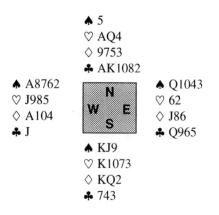

```
                    ♠ 5
                    ♡ AQ4
                    ◊ 9753
                    ♣ AK1082
  ♠ A8762                         ♠ Q1043
  ♡ J985          N               ♡ 62
  ◊ A104      W       E           ◊ J86
  ♣ J             S               ♣ Q965
                    ♠ KJ9
                    ♡ K1073
                    ◊ KQ2
                    ♣ 743
```

Post mortem

It was somewhat lucky to make this contract with all the cards but one (the ten of spades) badly placed. Ducking the club would not have been a good idea for West could play another spade and have enough tricks to defeat the contract on winning the ace of diamonds.

The truth: Cameron Small played this hand, as described above, on the internet.

Shortage of entries

The bidding

Sitting South in a knock-out teams match, I hold the following uninspiring collection at Game All:

♠ A874
♡ 94
◇ 852
♣ J762

My left-hand opponent opens one diamond, partner doubles and my right-hand opponent bids one heart. I have just enough to join in with one spade; in fact, a free bid of one spade describes my hand rather well. If East had passed and I had bid one spade, I could have held a Yarborough, but now I must have a few values or I would have taken the opportunity to pass. My left-hand opponent passes and partner raises me to four spades, ending the auction.

The bidding has been:

West	North	East	South
1 ◇	Dble	1 ♡	1 ♠
Pass	4 ♠	All Pass	

The play

West leads the seven of hearts and this is what I can see.

♠ KJ93
♡ AKQ
◇ KJ10
♣ Q103

♠ A874
♡ 94
◇ 852
♣ J762

I have three top losers, so it looks as if all will hinge on the trump suit. But, as is usually the case when the high-card values are unevenly divided, I must be careful about entries.

I see no reason to depart from the standard way of playing this spade suit for no loser. So, I must assume West has Qxx (or Qx) in spades. If that is the case I am going to draw trumps and end up with one trump in each of my two hands. I would like the larger of those two trumps to be in my hand – just in case I need an entry there later on. So at trick two I lead the nine of spades to my ace, a spade to dummy's jack which holds and cash the king of spades dropping West's queen. I now cash dummy's other two winning hearts, discarding a diamond. West discards two diamonds.

Now it looks as if West's original distribution was either 3-1-6-3 or 3-1-5-4. Presumably the club honours are split, or West may well have chosen to lead a top club at trick one. If clubs are 4-2 and I make the 'normal' play of leading the queen from the dummy, East will play his honour and continue with a second round of the suit. An astute West will duck this, putting me in the dummy. If I play a third club, West will win cheaply and play a fourth club, again putting me in the dummy and I will have to give him two diamond tricks.

Instead, I play a low club from the dummy. What can they do? If East plays high I can establish a second club trick. In practice, East plays low, I play the jack, and West has no answer. If he wins and plays a diamond I can afford to play the king (just in case East has the queen, though I am fairly sure it is with West), and now I play the queen of clubs. I must make ten tricks (five spades, three hearts, a diamond and a club). If instead West plays a club, now East must either lead a diamond or give me a ruff and discard.

The full deal:

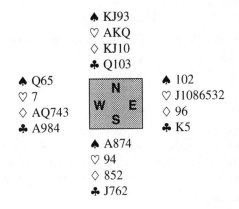

```
                    ♠ KJ93
                    ♡ AKQ
                    ◊ KJ10
                    ♣ Q103
      ♠ Q65                        ♠ 102
      ♡ 7                          ♡ J1086532
      ◊ AQ743                      ◊ 96
      ♣ A984                       ♣ K5
                    ♠ A874
                    ♡ 94
                    ◊ 852
                    ♣ J762
```

Post mortem

What if clubs had been 3-3? Now I am very glad I unblocked the nine of spades at trick two! The defenders cash two clubs and put me in dummy with the third round. But now I can come to hand with the eight of spades, cash my club trick and play a diamond to the king for my tenth trick.

The truth: This hand was played against me in a Young Chelsea Knock-out match. Declarer, an English international, played the queen of clubs from the dummy on the first round of the suit. My partner and I found the defence described above to beat the game.

Cross-ruff

The bidding

In fourth seat with everybody vulnerable I pick up as South:

♠ K
♡ K10864
◇ J743
♣ AJ9

My left-hand opponent passes and I hear partner open one club. East overcalls one spade and I bid a natural, forcing, two hearts. West joins in with two spades and partner raises to three hearts. I can't say I'm wild about my hand, but I don't like missing vulnerable games so I press on to four hearts.

The bidding has been:

West	North	East	South
Pass	1♣	1♠	2♡
2♠	3♡	Pass	4♡
All Pass			

The play

West leads the six of spades and this is what I can see:

♠ 7542
♡ AJ53
◇ K
♣ K873

	N	
W		E
	S	

♠ K
♡ K10864
◇ J743
♣ AJ9

East wins the ace of spades at trick one and returns the suit. There seems no merit in refusing to ruff, so I play the four of hearts and then lead a diamond towards dummy's king. West goes in with the ace and persists with a third round of spades.

It looks as if my best chance is some sort of cross-ruff. I can count on two club tricks, so I need eight trumps. That would be two spade ruffs in hand, three diamond ruffs in dummy, the ace of hearts in dummy and then maybe I can make both my king and ten of hearts, especially if East has the queen. To be able to ruff all my diamonds I need two entries to hand, so I will have to take a club finesse.

Accordingly, I ruff a diamond, cross to the jack of clubs, ruff a diamond, cross to the ace of clubs and ruff my last diamond. This is the position:

♠ 7
♡ A
♢ –
♣ K8

♠ –
♡ K108
♢ –
♣ 9

I have lost two tricks and made seven. The best chance looks to be to cash the ace of hearts and then play the king of clubs. I know that diamonds were 4-4 and that East started with five spades. I will be OK unless East was 5-2-4-2 without the queen of hearts. In that case he will ruff the king of clubs and promote a trick for West's queen of hearts by playing a spade. If that is the case there is nothing I can do.

So, I cash the ace of hearts and East shows out. Does that make any difference? No, all West has left is hearts. When I play a club he will have to ruff and lead into my king-ten of hearts.

The full deal:

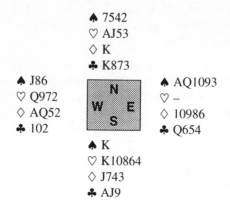

```
              ♠ 7542
              ♡ AJ53
              ◇ K
              ♣ K873
♠ J86                        ♠ AQ1093
♡ Q972          N            ♡ –
◇ AQ52      W       E        ◇ 10986
♣ 102           S            ♣ Q654
              ♠ K
              ♡ K10864
              ◇ J743
              ♣ AJ9
```

Post mortem

Given the precise lay-out of the diamonds, there are other successful lines. For example, I could have ruffed the third spade and laid down the king of hearts. When East shows out, I play the ten of hearts to the queen and king, and ruff a spade with my eight. After West overruffs, these cards are left:

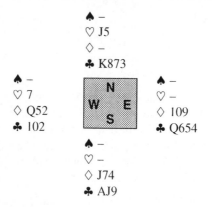

```
              ♠ –
              ♡ J5
              ◇ –
              ♣ K873
♠ –                          ♠ –
♡ 7             N            ♡ –
◇ Q52       W       E        ◇ 109
♣ 102           S            ♣ Q654
              ♠ –
              ♡ –
              ◇ J74
              ♣ AJ9
```

Suppose he exits with a trump. This squeezes East: a club discard gives four tricks in the suit, while if he discards a diamond, I play a club to the jack, and the jack of diamonds, pinning East's ten and setting up my seven as a winner.

The truth This deal occurred in the round robin of the 2001 World Juniors Teams championship. Lagas of the Netherlands was helped in finding a successful line by Grue for USAII opening two spades as East, showing spades and a minor.

Misleading declarer

The bidding

Sitting East at Game All in fourth position I pick up:

♠ K3
♥ AQ54
♦ K754
♣ 876

South on my left opens one spade, partner passes and North bids two clubs. It would not be sound to make a take-out double here, despite holding 12 HCP and four cards in each of the other two suits. When North has responded at the two level with a forcing bid in a new suit it is dangerous to enter the auction – unless your opponents have a fit, you won't have one either and could easily go for a large penalty.

Another reason for not doubling is that it is unlikely that your side will buy the hand, and if North or South end up as declarer, it is better not to give away information that can only help them.

So, I pass. South rebids two hearts and North jumps to four spades. The bidding has been:

West	North	East	South
–	–	–	1 ♠
Pass	2 ♣	Pass	2 ♥
Pass	4 ♠	All Pass	

The play

Partner leads the jack of diamonds and this is what I can see:

♠ QJ5
♡ J102
◇ A2
♣ KQ1043

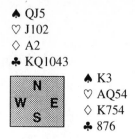

♠ K3
♡ AQ54
◇ K754
♣ 876

At trick one declarer plays low from the dummy and I win my king.

This does not look promising. There is no room for partner to hold a black-suit ace. If I leave declarer to his own devices, he will surely finesse my king of spades, and then my queen of hearts. I suppose we may come to a third defensive trick if partner has the ten of spades, but it is hard to see any prospect of a fourth.

I need to use my imagination and remember that declarer cannot see through the back of the cards. Just because I know the cards are lying well for him, does not mean that declarer knows it. Maybe I can persuade him that I have a doubleton heart. If I can do that he may not risk taking the spade finesse into partner's hand. That way I will make my king of spades and then I can give partner a heart ruff.

A low heart switch is no good because declarer will know I cannot have a low doubleton when partner does not win the queen. However, ace and another might work. The trouble with this is that declarer might feel he has to run the the second heart. If he rises with the king he will expect to go down most of the time that he has a spade loser; he may feel it is better odds to play me for the queen.

Ah, now I see it: I must switch to the queen of hearts…

Declarer plays the king, as I knew he would, and notes partner's play of the seven – I knew the top of his doubleton would look like an encouraging card. Declarer is now too frightened of a heart ruff to risk the spade finesse; instead he plays ace and another spade. I win with the king and play ace and another heart, giving partner a heart ruff for one down.

The full deal:

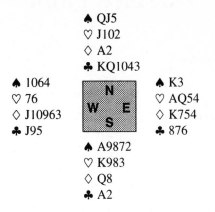

```
                    ♠ QJ5
                    ♡ J102
                    ◇ A2
                    ♣ KQ1043
       ♠ 1064                      ♠ K3
       ♡ 76            N           ♡ AQ54
       ◇ J10963     W     E        ◇ K754
       ♣ J95           S           ♣ 876
                    ♠ A9872
                    ♡ K983
                    ◇ Q8
                    ♣ A2
```

Post mortem

Note that declarer could have succeeded by winning the ace of diamonds at trick one and playing three rounds of clubs pitching a diamond. However, he was not to know that the clubs were behaving or that West had not led from the king of diamonds.

The truth: This deal was featured in 'Test Your Defence', a regular feature by Julian Pottage in *BRIDGE Magazine*.

Doubled game

The bidding

In first seat as South with the opponents vulnerable, I pick up a good hand:

♠ K54
♥ AK872
♦ 2
♣ AKJ5

I open one heart, which my partner raises to two. My right-hand opponent bids two spades and with the king of spades well placed my hand looks even better. I bid four hearts, which to my surprise is doubled on my left. It sounds like the suits will break badly so I refrain from redoubling.

The bidding has been:

West	North	East	South
–	–	–	1♡
Pass	2♡	2♠	4♡
Dble All Pass			

The play

West leads the queen of spades and this is what I can see:

♠ A73
♥ 1096
♦ J109753
♣ 6

♠ K54
♥ AK872
♦ 2
♣ AKJ5

The situation is not hopeless unless hearts are 5-0 but I have to take several ruffs in dummy – including a spade ruff once one has been discarded on the king of clubs. I must win the first spade in hand, so I can later play a second spade towards dummy's ace – that way, if West gets a spade ruff he will be ruffing my loser at the expense of a trump trick.

However, first I am going to play a diamond to cut the communications between the two defending hands. East wins the diamond and returns a trump (I am pleased he has one), which I win with the ace. As planned I now lead a spade on which West discards the king of diamonds. I win the ace of spades in dummy and take stock.

I can play the ace and king of clubs discarding a spade and ruff a spade but that leaves one trump in dummy for two club ruffs. Also, how do I get back to my hand without West overruffing and then removing dummy's last trump? It seems that I need the club finesse. But wait. East has six spades, one heart and, by the look of it, four diamonds. East probably has a doubleton club (certainly no more than three) so if he has the queen it will ruff down.

I cross to the ace of clubs, cash the king throwing a spade from dummy. The queen falls from East (he is 6-1-4-2) so I cash the jack of clubs and ruff a club in the dummy.

This is the position:

♠ –
♡ 10
◇ 10975
♣ –

♠ 5
♡ K872
◇ –
♣ –

If I ruff a diamond low West will overruff and return a low heart. I will be unable to get out of dummy without West making yet another trump trick and East must also make a spade.

The solution is to ruff the diamond with the king of hearts and play my last plain card, a spade. My trump pips are too good for West who can make no more than two trump tricks.

The full deal:

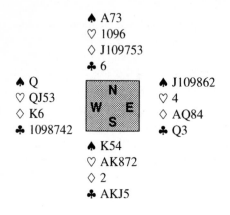

```
                    ♠ A73
                    ♡ 1096
                    ◊ J109753
                    ♣ 6
    ♠ Q                           ♠ J109862
    ♡ QJ53          N             ♡ 4
    ◊ K6        W       E         ◊ AQ84
    ♣ 1098742       S             ♣ Q3
                    ♠ K54
                    ♡ AK872
                    ◊ 2
                    ♣ AKJ5
```

Post mortem

Taking the club finesse was unnecessary and if it had been wrong I might have gone more down. There were two key plays: winning the spade in hand at trick one and ruffing the diamond high at the end.

The truth This is another hand from the semi-finals of the 2002 World Championship Women's Pairs in Montréal. Partner didn't quite get the timing right and went one down. The double should have made the hand easier to play.

Better than the finesse

The bidding

Sitting South at Love All, I hold the following interesting collection:

♠ 10
♡ 10
♢ A106542
♣ J10982

West, on my left, playing five-card majors, opens one spade and partner overcalls one no-trump. East bids a pre-emptive three spades and it is my turn.

It doesn't sound as if partner has too much in spades so we may have good chances of a minor-suit game. I could bid four no-trumps, asking partner to choose a minor, but this is often wrong when the longer suit is the higher, for with equal length partner will choose the lower. Here, if partner is 3-3 in the minors, I would certainly prefer to play in diamonds. I decide to settle for a simple four diamonds, which partner raises to five.

The bidding has been:

West	North	East	South
1 ♠	1NT	3 ♠	4 ♢
Pass	5 ♢	All Pass	

The play

West leads the ace of hearts and this is what I can see:

♠ AQ6
♡ J63
◇ J983
♣ AK7

♠ 10
♡ 10
◇ A106542
♣ J10982

On the ace of hearts, East encourages with the nine, and West continues with the king of hearts which I ruff.

Superficially, the contract depends simply on bringing in the club suit for no loser – a finesse through the opening bidder. But I wonder if I can improve my chances. If I could eliminate both major suits and exit with ace and another diamond, maybe I could endplay the player who won to open up clubs for me – either throwing East in to lead away from the queen of clubs, or else cashing the ace and king first and hoping that the hand with the doubleton diamond also held a doubleton club.

If I am going to try the endplay I will need to take the spade finesse. After my elimination and exit with a trump I will need at least one trump left in each hand or the defenders will simply exit in the majors. So I can ruff only three times in my hand, i.e. two hearts and one spade.

What do I think about the opponents' distribution? If West had five hearts as well as five spades he would probably have bid four spades (or four hearts) over my four diamonds. So it is probably East who has the five hearts. If that is the case, then both East and West have nine cards in the majors, so both must have four cards in the minors. Provided diamonds are 2-1 (which I must assume), then it is a certainty that the hand with the doubleton diamond has a doubleton club. I like this line more and more every minute!

After ruffing the second heart, I cash the ace of diamonds. West plays low while East plays the king. So now it looks as if West is the one who is 2-2 in the minors, so the queen of clubs could well be wrong. I continue with a spade to dummy's queen which holds. I now ruff my last heart, play a club to the king, cash the ace of spades, ruff a spade and cash the ace of clubs before exiting with a trump in this position:

♠ −
♡ −
◇ J9
♣ 7

♠ −
♡ −
◇ 10
♣ J10

West has only major-suit cards left, so I ruff his return in hand, as I pitch the seven of clubs from dummy.

The full deal:

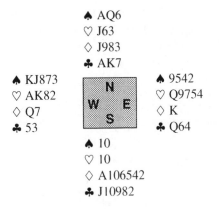

                        ♠ AQ6
                        ♡ J63
                        ◇ J983
                        ♣ AK7
    ♠ KJ873   ♠ 9542
    ♡ AK82   ♡ Q9754
    ◇ Q7   ◇ K
    ♣ 53   ♣ Q64
                        ♠ 10
                        ♡ 10
                        ◇ A106542
                        ♣ J10982

The truth: This hand was played like this by the German star Sabine Auken, albeit on a different, artificial, auction which started with a two spade opener by South showing a minor two-suiter. However, the inferences in the given and actual auctions were very similar.

Dreadful contract

The bidding

In fourth seat at Game All, I pick up a promising hand:

♠ A
♡ 543
◇ AQJ82
♣ AK52

My left-hand opponent opens three hearts, which is passed round to me. I have a very difficult decision. Double is out of the question because partner is bound to bid spades, while a simple overcall doesn't do justice to my values and overstates the suit. I decide to go for the throat and bid a gambling three no-trumps. Let's hope that partner has a heart stopper or that we have nine tricks if West doesn't lead a heart at trick one.

The bidding has been:

West	North	East	South
3♡	Pass	Pass	3NT
All Pass			

The play

West leads the eight of spades and this is what I can see:

♠ J7532
♡ 108
◇ 94
♣ J874

```
    N
  W   E
    S
```

♠ A
♡ 543
◇ AQJ82
♣ AK52

What a nightmare, and vulnerable too! I am pleased to have avoided a heart lead, but spades are not well stopped either.

Let's just hope to make as many tricks as possible. If the queen of clubs drops doubleton and the diamonds are 3-3 with the king onside I will make ten tricks, so at least there is some play for the contract.

I take my ace of spades and play the ace and king of clubs, West playing the queen on the second round. I lead a club to the jack and am about to take the diamond finesse when it strikes me that playing the nine sometimes tempts the defenders into making an error. With no particular reason in mind, I play the nine of diamonds; East covers with the ten and I follow with the jack, which holds the trick as West plays the five. I cross to dummy with the last club and play a diamond to my queen. Again I win the trick as West follows with the seven of diamonds.

I have seven tricks in the bag and could cash the ace of diamonds for eight, or ten if the king drops. If the seven of diamonds is an honest card the diamonds aren't breaking. I stop to consider my options. It is likely that, given the vulnerability, West has seven hearts and is therefore 2-7-2-2. If his hearts had been sequential he would have led one, so East has a singleton king or queen! The position would be:

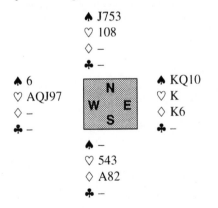

```
                    ♠ J753
                    ♡ 108
                    ◇ –
                    ♣ –
    ♠ 6                         ♠ KQ10
    ♡ AQJ97          N          ♡ K
    ◇ –           W     E       ◇ K6
    ♣ –              S          ♣ –
                    ♠ –
                    ♡ 543
                    ◇ A82
                    ♣ –
```

I decide to see whether West knows what is going on and lead the three of hearts. Time stands still but eventually West plays the jack of hearts, which East has to overtake with the king. After cashing his two spade tricks East can give dummy two spade tricks or play a diamond allowing me to finesse the eight. I have made a most fortunate ten tricks.

The full deal:

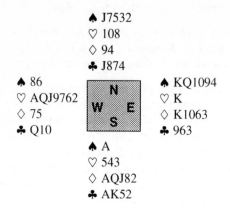

```
                 ♠ J7532
                 ♡ 108
                 ◇ 94
                 ♣ J874
   ♠ 86                          ♠ KQ1094
   ♡ AQJ9762        N            ♡ K
   ◇ 75          W     E         ◇ K1063
   ♣ Q10            S            ♣ 963
                 ♠ A
                 ♡ 543
                 ◇ AQJ82
                 ♣ AK52
```

Post mortem

Three no-trumps was a wild bid which I was very lucky to get away
although any other bid is likely to lead to a minus score, possibly doubled.
It is seems impossible to reach a contract of four clubs. West did well to
avoid the lead of the queen of hearts but should he have got it right later?
If I had had Kxx in hearts he would have done the right thing.

The truth: East/West were playing for the Indonesian team which reached the final
of the Rosenblum in the 2002 World Championships, losing to the Italian Lavazza
team. Our hero who brought home the contract in a round-robin match was
England's Phil King.

The devil's work

The bidding

First in hand with both sides vulnerable I pick up:

♠ K8
♡ K952
◇ QJ84
♣ A106

I open one no-trump (12–14) and, after West passes, North bids two clubs, Stayman. I show him my four-card heart suit, he raises me to three hearts and I press on to game.

The bidding has been:

West	North	East	South
–	–	–	1NT
Pass	2♣	Pass	2♡
Pass	3♡	Pass	4♡
All Pass			

The play

West leads the two of clubs and partner puts down an uninspiring dummy:

♠ QJ96
♡ A1073
◇ 106
♣ K84

♠ K8
♡ K952
◇ QJ84
♣ A106

Quite why partner thought he was worth issuing a game invitation on a balanced 10-count facing a weak no-trump, I do not know. Game seems to have little play. With two top diamonds and a spade to lose, my only chance is to play trumps for no loser. I suppose I might succeed if East held a singleton honour, but perhaps a better chance is to play for a Devil's Coup. In this play the opposing trump honours need to be split and the suit must break 3-2. In addition I will need a specific distribution of the side suits.

Still, I have never executed a Devil's Coup at the table and it has always been a minor ambition to do so. The first task is to lose all my inevitable top losers.

I play low from dummy to the first trick and win East's queen with my ace. The king of spades loses to East's ace (West playing the five). East switches to the three of diamonds won by West's king and West plays a second spade, the two, which I win in the dummy to play another diamond. East wins with the ace and plays another diamond. I play the queen from hand, and West and dummy both discard clubs. This is the position:

♠ J9
♡ A1073
◇ –
♣ K

♠ –
♡ K952
◇ J
♣ 106

I need to decide who has the long hearts, and it seems to be West. His carding suggests he started with four spades; I know he began with only two diamonds; and by leading the two of clubs he suggested four cards in that suit. If he has the long trumps I need to reach an end position where in hand I have K9 of trumps and a plain card, while in dummy I have A107 of trumps. And that plain card must be in a suit in which East still has a card.

To that end I play a club to the king, ruff a spade, ruff a club and ruff a spade. On this last spade ruff East discards a diamond, so it looks as if my count of the hand is correct. These are the last three cards with the lead in my hand:

```
          ♠ –
          ♡ A107
          ◇ –
          ♣ –
♠ –                        ♠ –
♡ Q84        [N W E S]     ♡ J6
◇ –                        ◇ 9
♣ –                        ♣ –
          ♠ –
          ♡ K9
          ◇ J
          ♣ –
```

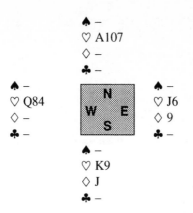

Now I play the jack of diamonds. If West ruffs low I overruff with the ten and make the last two tricks with the ace and king of trumps. His best shot is to ruff with the queen, but now I overruff with the ace and finesse East for the jack of hearts on the way back.

The full deal:

```
              ♠ QJ96
              ♡ A1073
              ◇ 106
              ♣ K84
♠ 10532                        ♠ A74
♡ Q84          [N W E S]       ♡ J6
◇ K7                           ◇ A9532
♣ J952                         ♣ Q73
              ♠ K8
              ♡ K952
              ◇ QJ84
              ♣ A106
```

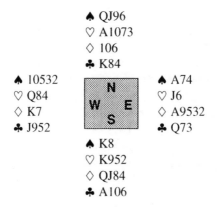

Post mortem

Do you see West's error? When East played a third round of diamonds, West should have discarded a spade, not a club. Now declarer can never reach the required end position.

The truth: I have yet to realise my ambition of playing a Devil's Coup at the table. The deal was played by one of my ex-partners, Steve Lodge, in the Schiphol tournament in the Netherlands.

False sense of security

The bidding

Sitting East at Game All in fourth position, I am looking at:

♠ 976
♡ K109842
♢ 5
♣ KQ4

South on my left opens one spade, partner passes and North responds two hearts. That ends any hankering I may have had to enter the auction, so I pass and South rebids three clubs, a natural bid showing extra values. North now closes the auction with four spades and everybody passes.

The bidding has been:

West	North	East	South
–	–	–	1♠
Pass	2♡	Pass	3♣
Pass	4♠	All Pass	

The play

Partner leads the queen of diamonds and this is what I can see:

♠ A103
♡ AQJ5
♢ 763
♣ 965

	N	
W		E
	S	

♠ 976
♡ K109842
♢ 5
♣ KQ4

Defensive prospects look remote here. Declarer surely has five spade tricks, two hearts (once he has knocked out my king), the ace and king of diamonds, and the ace of clubs. It seems as if desperate measures are called for.

Declarer wins trick one with the king of diamonds and plays a heart to dummy's queen. If I win this trick, surely declarer will soon be claiming his contract. So I duck smoothly! Declarer is now confident of ten tricks. He discards a diamond on the ace of hearts and can surely not lose more than three black-suit tricks. Maybe he can ruff his fourth club in the dummy, which may be necessary if trumps are 4-1. So, at trick four declarer plays the ace of clubs followed by another club. I am in with the queen and casually play a heart. Declarer 'knows' it is safe to ruff low for West is marked with the king of hearts. Partner overruffs the heart, gives me a diamond ruff and I cash the king of clubs for one down.

The full deal:

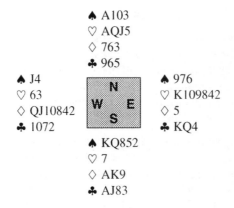

               ♠ A103
               ♡ AQJ5
               ◊ 763
               ♣ 965

♠ J4   ♠ 976
♡ 63   ♡ K109842
◊ QJ10842   ◊ 5
♣ 1072   ♣ KQ4

               ♠ KQ852
               ♡ 7
               ◊ AK9
               ♣ AJ83

Post mortem

Did declarer play badly? Once two hearts have lived and he has got his discard, it seemed to him that his only danger was a bad spade break in addition to a poor lie in clubs. His club play looks reasonable because he may need to ruff the fourth round of the suit in the dummy. Surely any declarer would have gone down after my brilliant defence.

The truth No, again this wasn't me, but English international and top-class rubber bridge player, Gunnar Hallberg. And it didn't quite go like that at the table either. Although Gunnar defended exactly as described, his superstar partner was dozing and forgot to give him a diamond ruff!

A Norwegian would

The bidding

Sitting South, in second seat at Love All, I pick up:

♠ 9
♡ AJ103
♢ A432
♣ K976

I really dislike 4-4-4-1 hands, because they are difficult to evaluate. And I never know whether to keep bidding my suits when partner bids my singleton, or rebid no-trumps. Still, today I am playing five-card majors and a strong no-trump. So I will open one club, which maximises my chance of finding a fit, and risk a one no-trump rebid with my singleton if partner responds one spade.

I am pleasantly surprised when my partner responds two clubs. We play 'inverted minor raises', so this bid is forcing for one round and shows at least four clubs. If I had a balanced hand I would rebid two no-trumps, but otherwise I bid naturally. So, I bid two diamonds and partner continues with two hearts. The original two club bid denies a four-card major so this just shows something in hearts and asks me to continue to describe my hand. That's easy. I raise to three hearts.

Partner now bids four clubs, setting the suit for slam purposes and asking me to cue-bid. I bid four diamonds and this encourages partner into bidding four no-trumps, Roman Key Card Blackwood. I bid five diamonds to show zero or three aces out of the five (the king of clubs counts as an ace). Partner presses on with five hearts, asking about the queen of trumps, and I sign off in six clubs.

It has been a long auction:

West	North	East	South
–	–	–	1♣
Pass	2♣	Pass	2◇
Pass	2♡	Pass	3♡
Pass	4♣	Pass	4◇
Pass	4NT	Pass	5◇
Pass	5♡	Pass	6♣
All Pass			

The play

After quite a pause West leads the queen of spades, and I await the sight of dummy with some anticipation:

♠ AKJ
♡ K72
◇ Q76
♣ A1042

♠ 9
♡ AJ103
◇ A432
♣ K976

Partner seems to have got somewhat carried away. I was not aware that I had shown any extra values and he has forced me to a small slam with a balanced 17-count including what he knew was a 'wasted' king of spades. I suppose he would have thought I had a five-card club suit, but even so...

Still, the slam has some play. I need to get to a position where I have played off all my major-suit cards (guessing the position of the queen of hearts in the process) and then perhaps I can throw someone in with a trump to lead away from the king of diamonds. West has made a slightly strange opening lead, after quite a pause, and I am inclined to place him with most of the outstanding high cards.

I win the ace of spades and play a low club from the dummy. East plays the jack. I win the king. If East's jack of clubs is a singleton I'm sure I can't make my contract – it is going to be hard enough on a 3-2 club break. So I play a club back to the ace and both opponents follow. At least now I know who has the master trump – East would not have played the jack of clubs from jack doubleton as that would have allowed me to pick up the trump suit for no loss. I now cash my king and jack of spades pitching two diamonds from hand. West shows out on the third round, discarding a diamond.

So I know that East began with seven spades and three clubs which makes it likely that it is West who holds the queen of hearts. I play a heart to my ace and run the jack of hearts which holds the trick with both opponents following.

Now I have to guess whether East's remaining unknown card is a heart or a diamond. If East is void of diamonds it would give West a six-card suit and he may well have made a weak jump overcall over my one club opening. I am going to play East for an original 7-2-1-3 distribution.

Accordingly, I cash the ace of diamonds and exit with a trump. This is the position:

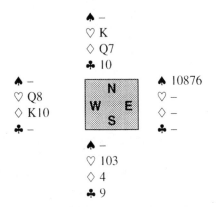

East perforce plays a spade. I discard a diamond from hand and West has an insoluble problem. If he discards a heart I ruff the spade in dummy, cash the king of hearts and my hand is high. If he discards a diamond, after I have ruffed the spade in dummy, I ruff a diamond in hand and dummy is high.

The full deal:

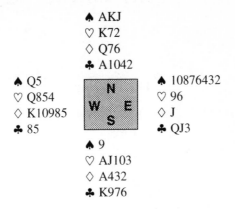

                    ♠ AKJ
                    ♡ K72
                    ◇ Q76
                    ♣ A1042

    ♠ Q5   ♠ 10876432
    ♡ Q854   ♡ 96
    ◇ K10985   ◇ J
    ♣ 85   ♣ QJ3

                    ♠ 9
                    ♡ AJ103
                    ◇ A432
                    ♣ K976

Post mortem

East's play of the jack of clubs on the first round of trumps was a real give-away. It is the sort of play that is often made because 'it cannot cost' but here it told declarer who had the master trump. Without such information he would probably have played West for the trump length (because of the known disparity of spade length). Declarer might well have gone wrong.

If you think about, it is a virtual impossibility that declarer is going to duck that first round of trumps, so playing the jack is unlikely ever to gain.

The truth: This deal occurred in the Norwegian Open Championship and was reported by Tommy Sandsmark. The declarer, who succeeded at the table, was Jan Einar Saetre.

Low point-count slam

The bidding

First in hand at Game All, I pick up the following:

♠ 753
♡ 6
◇ AKQ87
♣ J753

I am a committed light opener (I get more value for my table money if I bid a lot) so I open an unsound one diamond. Four spades on my left, four no-trumps from partner, pass on my right. I think partner wants me to bid a new suit. so I try five clubs. West, rather surprisingly, presses on with five spades, and partner gives me six clubs, which ends the auction.

West	North	East	South
–	–	–	1◇
4♠	4NT	Pass	5♣
5♠	6♣	All Pass	

The play

West leads the king of spades and partner tables his dummy:

♠ –
♡ AJ10752
◇ 94
♣ K10864

♠ 753
♡ 6
◇ AKQ87
♣ J753

I see that I have a lot of work to do. A slam on only 19 HCP and no great fit! That will teach me for opening so light. This would not be a great contract at the best of times, but West's bidding suggests that suits will be breaking badly.

I realise at once that I probably need trumps to break 2-2; if West has singleton ace or a singleton small card I have two trump losers anyway, while if he has singleton queen I will find it hard to do all the ruffing necessary without losing a trick to East's nine. So, I need trumps 2-2 with West having one honour. Is that more likely to be the ace or queen?

In my view it is more likely to be the ace. He undoubtedly has eight spades but he needs something else for a voluntary vulnerable five spade bid. That something is probably a sure trick and the ace of clubs is the only one he can have. In addition, had he held Qx of clubs he would perhaps hope to score a trick in defence, and thus, again, the five spade bid would have been less attractive.

So it seems as if I have ten tricks: four trumps in dummy plus two ruffs in hand, along with three diamonds and a heart. If West has ten cards in the black suits neither of the red suits is likely to break. Maybe he has a doubleton honour in hearts so I can establish the suit by ruffing one and then taking a ruffing finesse; if not I will need some sort of squeeze. If I am to have any chance of establishing hearts I need to play on that suit immediately.

So, I ruff the spade, cash the ace of hearts and ruff a heart. West follows twice, with the four and the nine. I now play a club to dummy's king, which holds, and a second club. West wins the ace and continues spades. These cards remain with the lead in dummy:

♠ —
♡ J1075
◇ 94
♣ 10

```
    N
  W   E
    S
```

♠ 7
♡ —
◇ AKQ87
♣ J

West plays another spade. I ruff in the dummy as East follows suit.

Unless by some miracle hearts are 3-3, I can't establish the suit, partly because I don't have enough entries, but also because I don't have enough trumps. However, if West has a doubleton heart then he probably has a singleton diamond (I know he has two clubs, and eight spades seems likely); if that is the case I have to decide whether that singleton is an honour (jack or ten) or a small card. As there are only two honours and four small cards, it is better odds to play him for a small diamond, in which case I need to take a diamond finesse now. Of course, if hearts are 3-3, then West has a void diamond, in which case a diamond finesse is bound to succeed.

I play the nine of diamonds from the dummy. East plays low and West follows with the six. I now ruff a heart and ruff a spade, but East is squeezed on this trick. He cannot keep J10xx of diamonds and his top heart.

The full deal:

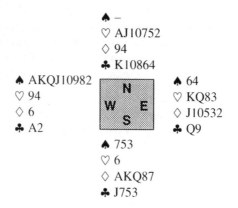

```
                    ♠ –
                    ♡ AJ10752
                    ◇ 94
                    ♣ K10864
♠ AKQJ10982                          ♠ 64
♡ 94              ┌──────────┐       ♡ KQ83
◇ 6              │    N     │       ◇ J10532
♣ A2             │  W    E  │       ♣ Q9
                 │    S     │
                 └──────────┘
                    ♠ 753
                    ♡ 6
                    ◇ AKQ87
                    ♣ J753
```

Post mortem

Can you see East's error? He should have covered the nine of diamonds. I win in hand and ruff a spade, but now I am dummy in this position:

♠ –
♡ J1075
◊ 4
♣ –

♠
♡ –
◊ AK87
♣ J

I cannot cash my last club and East is under no pressure. He can keep four diamonds and a top heart.

It looks as if I misplayed after all. Despite the two to one odds in my favour of finding West with a singleton small diamond, I should have played him for the singleton ten or jack. What I should have done after ruffing West's spade in this position:

♠ –
♡ J1075
◊ 94
♣ 10

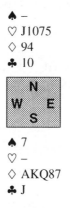

♠ 7
♡ –
◊ AKQ87
♣ J

was to ruff a heart and cash the ace of diamonds unblocking dummy's nine (West's ten dropping, say). Now when I ruff my last spade with dummy's last club, East is again squeezed in the red suits.

The truth: No, I'm afraid I didn't play the hand as well as that at the table. In real life I was quickly down after crossing to a diamond at trick two (I did play the nine to the ace) and playing a club to the ten.

Wrong contract

The bidding

Sitting South at Love All, my left-hand opponent opens three clubs. Partner doubles for take-out and it is my turn:

♠ AJ72
♡ 106
◇ 753
♣ AJ73

It seems that I have four choices: pass, three spades, four spades and three no-trumps. First, I rule out bidding any number of spades; three spades is something of an underbid while four spades could be too high, and in any event there is no guarantee that partner holds more than three cards in the suit. At Love All it is tempting to pass but eventually I decide to go by Hamman's Rule: when three no-trumps is a sensible option, bid it.

The bidding has been:

West	North	East	South
3♣	Dble	Pass	3NT
All Pass			

The play

West leads the eight of spades and dummy puts down:

♠ K10964
♡ A832
◇ AQ6
♣ 10

	N	
W		E
	S	

♠ AJ72
♡ 106
◇ 753
♣ AJ73

Oh dear, it looks very much as if I have done the wrong thing. Four spades seems cold, and if spades are 2-2, as looks very likely on the lead, then three clubs doubled would have gone for at least 300. In three no-trumps, on the other hand, it is not clear how I am going to arrive at more than eight tricks.

Let's start by making a few assumptions: spades are probably 2-2 and the king of diamonds is almost certainly wrong. There are several possibilities for my ninth trick. First, I may be able to eliminate the black suits and throw East in with a heart to lead into dummy's diamonds. Alternatively, I may be able to eliminate the red suits and endplay West in clubs.

If West has led a doubleton spade, there is a strong inference that he is 2-2-2-7, for with a three-card side suit he would probably have preferred that as a lead.

I want to start attacking my opponents' communications, so I play the ten of spades from dummy, which holds, and lead a low heart.

East goes in with the queen of hearts (West playing the nine) and switches to the nine of clubs. If I was certain that West was 2-2-2-7 there is an easy route home. All I need to do is win the ace of clubs, run the spades and exit in hearts. But there are other ways home when that is the situation and I don't have to commit to it now.

I play low on the club, hoping that West will win and continue spades, which will give me more time to test other prospects. But West is on form and switches to the eight of diamonds, breaking up my position in that suit. His defence is not good enough, however.

I duck the eight of diamonds, which holds. He continues with another diamond which I win with the ace. Now I cash the ace of hearts followed by *two* more spades and exit with the jack of clubs. West, with only clubs left, has to win the queen and lead into my ace-seven. I gratefully cash my two club tricks and two more spades for my contract.

The full deal:

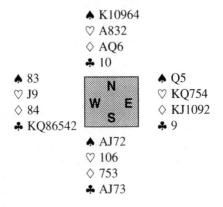

```
                   ♠ K10964
                   ♡ A832
                   ◇ AQ6
                   ♣ 10
     ♠ 83                      ♠ Q5
     ♡ J9          N           ♡ KQ754
     ◇ 84       W     E        ◇ KJ1092
     ♣ KQ86542     S           ♣ 9
                   ♠ AJ72
                   ♡ 106
                   ◇ 753
                   ♣ AJ73
```

Post mortem

In truth, there were several successful lines. The key play was the early play of ducking a heart to sever communications between the East and West hands.

The truth: Having started with a hand on which I succeeded, I thought I'd finish in the same vein. The line described above is the one I took at the table. I thought I would to lose 1 IMP when opponents at the other table made four spades, but in the other room West passed and North opened one spade. East overcalled two spades showing 5-5 in hearts and a minor. This caused North to misguess spades in the eventual contract of four spades and he went one down (though, looking at all four hands, there are plenty of ways for declarer to succeed even after losing a spade trick).